Closing the Deal

A Handbook for Maximising Value in Business Disposals

By Nick Matthews

CONTENTS

ABOUT THE AUTHOR		3
1.	FOREWORD	4
2.	DISPOSAL PROCESS AT A GLANCE	8
3.	PREPARING FOR A DISPOSAL	10
4.	VALUATION	36
5.	MARKETING DOCUMENTATION FOR THE INDICATIVE OFFER PHASE	48
6.	THE VENDOR DUE DILIGENCE	74
7.	THE NON-BINDING INDICATIVE OFFER PHASE, COMMUNICATION WITH BIDDERS AND MNAGING THE CONTACT PROGRAM	81
8.	THE DUE DILIGENCE PHASE	98
9.	CLOSING THE DEAL	126
10.	LEGAL CONSIDERATIONS	132
GLOSSARY OF M&A TERMINOLOGY		143
ANNEXURE: DATA ROOM CHECKLIST		155

About the Author

Nick Matthews is Head of Deal Advisory and a Partner at

KPMG in South Africa. During his 20-year career at KPMG, Nick has advised on a broad range of mid-market disposals of South African, Mauritian, Zambian, Kenyan, Motswana, and Tanzanian businesses. These businesses have operated in the Mining, Banking, Insurance, Retail, Manufacturing, Services, Packaging, Logistics, Health Care, Pharmaceutical, and Aerospace and Defense sectors.

Clients have included Multinational Corporations, Governments, Private Equity Firms, and Owner Managers.

A large proportion of these transactions have been cross border in nature, dealing with sellers and buyers from Australia, Germany, France, UK, US, Japan, China, and across Africa. In this regard Nick has worked extensively with the global KPMG M&A network in delivering M&A solutions to KPMG's global clients.

In addition to executing on M&A transactions, which includes buy side advice, Nick has developed and is responsible for the KPMG network's global M&A training program.

Nick is married with two children, and lives in Johannesburg, South Africa. When not advising on Mergers and Acquisitions, Nick spends time with his family, often on the golf course.

1. Foreword

Over the author's 20-year career as an investment banker, a large proportion of services provided have involved running competitive auction disposal processes, predominantly in the mid-market where the author's firm, KPMG, is a global leader. The author has witnessed a genesis in M&A (Mergers and Acquisitions) advisory services whereby new products and services have been introduced - such as the Virtual Data Room, the Vendor Due Diligence, Locked-Box completion, and more recently Warranty and Indemnity Insurance. In an age where there is an increasing propensity for sector focused advisors, the author has, notwithstanding had the opportunity to advise on a broad range of sectors, for which he is grateful.

The author's work includes running sale processes for owner managers and family businesses, but the author's clients are also corporates, multi-nationals, and private equity firms. The author's clients range from sophisticated professionally run firms who are serial transactors, with highly developed in-house M&A capability, to entrepreneurial organizations with very little knowledge of the M&A process.

Businesses the author has been mandated to sell have been based in South Africa, Mauritius, Tanzania, Zambia, Kenya and Botswana. In addition to advising sellers located in the author's home town of Johannesburg, South Africa, my firm's global reach, has meant that the author has been fortunate to be mandated by sellers from France, Germany, Greece, United Kingdom, and Australia. Similarly, I have dealt with buyers from across the globe, including South Africa, Congo Brazzaville, Mauritius, Ghana, France, Turkey, Russia, China, United Kingdom, and the United States. Through my firm, the author has also had the opportunity to work with other KPMG investment bankers around the world, which has been a valuable learning source through which he has been able to hone my investment banking skills.

On a recent business trip, the author was advising a client in the preparation for a management presentation in Cape Town, and on the return flight back to Johannesburg decided it would be useful to prepare an aide memoire - the do's and don'ts of a management presentation. That thought lead him to consider writing this book – a handbook for managing a disposal process.

The book is not intended to be a comprehensive guide to all aspects of M&A, the author does not purport to be a competent legal, or tax advisor. Although we have a chapter on valuation considerations, which are important to any M&A process, the comprehensive subject of business valuations is also beyond the scope of this book.

This book is, however intended to be a reference for M&A practitioners, business development professionals managing sale processes, Private equity fund managers and owners considering a sale of their own business. The author is often finding himself repeating my advice to his staff, and to his clients, and feel there is also value to young professionals in putting the author's thoughts and knowledge into words.

Importantly, this book is not meant for academic reference, it is written based on learnings from practical experience. The author tried to include real life 'war stories' to augment his writing. There has been limited research into this book, the author does not have the time or propensity for this. However, he does not believe that is required for a practical handbook such as this.

Included in the book is a detailed glossary of terms, which it is hoped will be a useful reference point to those looking for a single reference point to demystify M&A terminology and jargon. The KPMG publication 'M&A Jargon Demystified', has been a useful reference in preparing the glossary. Also included as an appendix is a typical information request list, this type of list can be used to populate a data room. Thanks is due to Boitumelo Ngutshane, Head of Transaction Services at KPMG in South Africa, who provided this.

A special word of thanks is required for some subject matter experts who provided some input and commentary on this first draft, in particular thanks are due to Jameel Nagdee, of Investec Bank, who reviewed and commented on the Stapled Debt section of chapter 5.

The author also hopes this will be a useful read and reference for an investment banker embarking on his or her career, and also for a seller keen to better understand the management process of a typical sell side auction.

Nick Matthews
June 2018

2. Disposal Process at a Glance

Every disposal process is unique, and timelines should be tailored for the particular circumstances for each business disposal. However, the process envisaged in this book follows the typical process flow as set out below.

Factors which affect timing include:
- The sellers governance processes and approvals required to approve documentation and decisions at key steps along the way (for example approval of the Information Memorandum, approval of long list of buyers, approval of shortlisted bidders, etc.);
- Availability of information, particularly during the preparation phase;
- Timing of financial year end, and completion of audited accounts, which can impact on the start of the disposal process;
- Complexity of the business,
- The nature and extent of negotiations which can have a significant impact on the timing of the completion phase, and
- Regulatory approval processes which can have a significant delay on the implementation of a signed sale agreement.

Notwithstanding these factors, this book follows the structure of a typical sale process, and we have included a process flow below, which is referenced to parts of this book.

Phase I

PLANNING (3-4 weeks)

- Engage with management to:
  - Prepare financial projections and business plan (page 31)
  - Understand the key business drivers and growth potential
- Valuation (Chapter 4)
  - Prepare indicative price range (relative pricing and DCF)
  - Assist in decision on floor price
  - Advice on pricing and further steps
  - Assess key impacts to valuation
- Determine the strategy for the disposal and preliminary research of buyers (pages 11, 25)
- Provide tax considerations for exiting shareholders

SALE PREPARATION (4-6 weeks)

- Preparation of NDA, Teaser and Information Memorandum (Chapter 5)
- Finalize list of potential parties to approach (page 24)
- Prepare data room for Due Diligence
- Consider appropriateness of Vendor Due Diligence (Chapter 6):
  - Limits the need for multiple DDs to be carried out
  - Limits access to seller's sensitive information
  - Allows seller more control over the sale process
  - Allows seller to deal with potential issues upfront
- Consider warranty insurance (page 138)

Full Disposal Process (Phase II)

COMPETITIVE AUCTION

Non-binding Indicative Offer Phase (Chapter 5) — 3-4 weeks

- Approach parties on a limited basis and circulate teaser (page 93)
- Execute non-disclosure agreements with potential parties and distribute Information Memorandum (pages 48, 93, 95)
- Circulate Information Memorandum
- Prepare Management presentations (page 57, 95)
- Receive and evaluate Non-binding Indicative Offers (page 97)
- Short list bidders to next stage (page 98)
- Advise shortlisted bidders on the timetable (Process Letter 2 - page 104)

Due Diligence Phase (Chapter 8) — 6-8 weeks

- Provide full access to data room (page 107, 112)
- Management Presentations (page 116)
- Conduct site visits (page 106)
- Facilitating Q&A with bidders (page 107)
- Receive and evaluate binding offers (Chapter 9)
- Shortlist final bidders (page 126)

Negotiations (page 130) — 4 weeks

- Negotiate pricing and other commercial terms
- Firm up final offers and marked up Agreements
- Select best final offer for exclusivity and final negotiations

EXCLUSIVITY & CLOSING (6-10 weeks)

- Continue final negotiations until successful closing
- Finalise SPA and other transaction documents (Chapter 10)
- Fulfil conditions to closing (accounting, legal, etc.) (page 137)
- Completion

3. Preparing for a Disposal Process

When to embark on a co-ordinated, competitive disposal process

Often in the author's career he has come across business owners who have entered bilateral negotiations with an aspirant purchaser. Some of these have been a resounding success, but often, a significant amount of time an effort has been expensed to find that the proposed transaction comes to naught. This can, and often is, followed by further exclusive negotiations with another party, but once again the seller runs the risk of these discussions coming to nothing. The competitive auction process greatly reduces the risk of failure in a transaction by concurrently progressing discussions with multiple parties, limiting the risk of failure with one party.

Situations where exclusive bilateral negotiations are appropriate

There are, however, situations where there is a clear and obvious buyer for a business, and there is unlikely to be any value derived from a competitive auction process. An example of this would include where a business is an exclusive agent for its principles product, and any transaction would require approval by the licensor. In such circumstance, it may make sense to enter exclusive discussions with one's supplier. Other than these limited circumstances, where the buyer is an obvious and exclusive choice, a competitive auction is likely to increase value, and reduce the risk of transaction failure. The real problem in entering bilateral discussions is that, although one can make some inferences about the veracity of a proposed buyer, one never knows if they will ultimately close the deal. Although the competitive auction involves more set up and preparation time, and costs to the seller, it is more likely to result in a successful transaction, and in a higher price by maintaining the competitive tension and eliminative speculative and non-committal buyers along the way.

Of course, in discussing a proposed competitive auction sale process with potential buyers, one will often receive negative feedback, particularly from private equity firms. Their overwhelming preference is for bilateral discussions, as they are more likely to close a 'sweetheart deal.' However, most buyers, if they are really keen, will endure the frustration of being in a competitive process. In addition, although they will know they are up against other bidders, they generally appreciate the preparation that is made to facilitate Due Diligence, and the value associated with a well-prepared information memorandum. Hiring sell side advisors, and the initiation of a formal process also demonstrates intent by the seller, with the concomitant commitment to costs, etc.

CASE STUDY: When Bilateral Negotiations are Appropriate

In 2015, the author was approached by the board of a bank holding company to advise on the sale of their captive credit life insurance company used by the group to provide credit life insurance to the customers of their bank. The bank had been placed into receivership following a loss of confidence, and the Receiver was in the process of separating out a 'Good Bank' which would be recapitalized and would recommence business. Due to the nature of the laws around receivership, only the bank could be placed into receivership. However, the highly profitable credit life insurance business remained under control of the separately listed holding company. To prepare a compelling and profitable business plan, it was important for the Receiver to gain control of the credit life book for all the loans associated with the Good Bank.

The nature of the operations of the credit life insurer, and that of the bank, were intricately intertwined as the only source of business for the insurer was the bank. Accordingly, whilst it was theoretically conceivable that a third party would be able to purchase and manage the credit insurance run-off, there was much more value to the bank in purchasing the book, and the value difference between what the credit insurer was worth to Good Bank, and what it would be worth to a third party was considerable.

Under these circumstances, the running of a competitive auction process would prove futile. The real challenge was to ensure that value was maximized for the bank holding company and its shareholders, given the lack of competitive tension. In this case detailed financial modelling, and valuation becomes critical to ensure that as the sell side advisors you can maximize value for the seller without reference to the benefits associated with competing bidders driving up price.

Minority shareholder rights and how these affects the competitive disposal process

It is often the case in private company shareholder agreements, that there is a first right of refusal offered between shareholders. This is also often referred to as a pre-emptive right. The nature of a first right of refusal is that it obliges the shareholders, to offer other shareholders, the right to purchase the selling shareholder's stake in a company on the same terms and conditions which may have been offered by any other third party. It often accompanied by tag along rights providing the minority shareholder the right to insist that his interest in the company is purchased on the same terms and conditions as offered to the majority shareholder. Whilst on the face of it, a first right of refusal does not restrict a majority shareholder from offering his shares for sale, it represents a major frustration to any buyer as they will never be sure if the carpet will be pulled from underneath them once finally concluding a transaction with the majority shareholder. It would be disingenuous for any seller to conceal such an arrangement from prospective buyers, and probably impossible to do so through any Due Diligence process.

The best approach is therefore be to engage with the other shareholder (i.e. the shareholder holding the first right of refusal), either to procure the waiver of this right, or alternatively determine a reserve price, above which they would not exercise their rights. Ultimately the party holding the first right of refusal may not agree to such an arrangement, in which case the best course of action would be to offer potential bidders a break fee to compensate them in the event that the minority shareholders exercise their pre-emptive right.

Such a break fee would need to be meaningful, not only to cover the cost of any external advice paid for by the selected bidder, but also the cost of their own senior executives' time, as well as any hassle factor. This fee would then become payable, if a transaction is concluded with a particular bidder, only to be scuppered through the minority shareholder exercising their pre-emptive first right of refusal.

Selection of a lead M&A advisor

In selling a business through a competitive process, an M&A advisor is essential. Many larger multinational corporates have in-house M&A (sometimes referred to as Business Development) teams. These Business Development professionals often come out of investment banks and therefore often have a sound knowledge of a typical disposal process. Even a dedicated in-house team, though, would typically require the assistance of external advisors, especially where the business disposal is in a different country, and where global buyers are sought.

In looking for a lead M&A advisor, the following are some of the key attributes one should consider:

Access to buyers

A key feature of an advisor is the ability, through the advisor firms' network to access global buyers, particularly in cross border transactions, where the seller is located in a different country (or continent) from the asset being disposed.

Being able to call on professionals in the sellers' geography who have access to, and relationship with buyers there, is critical to ensure the opportunity is appropriately pitched within each buyers' organization. If looking for buyers around the world, a global presence will be critical to open doors wherever buyers may be. This place the 'Big Four' accounting firms, and to a lesser extent the global investment banks, at a distinct advantage over local niche advisory boutiques.

Cross border considerations

When a global multinational is looking to sell a business in a different country, it is often useful to have an advisor with a presence in the country of the seller, and also a presence in a country where the assets are based. In any sale process, having on-the-ground professionals to manage interactions with the management team is critical. In addition, sellers are often comfortable dealing with an advisor in their home town or country who can interface with the seller in their home market. This is particularly important where there are cultural and language barriers which need to be managed between the two countries.

Senior team involvement

Depending on the size of transaction, consideration should be given to just how significant the mandate will be to the advisory firm. One should ensure that the individual leading the pitch, if he is a key factor in the appointment decision, is going to be the individual leading the execution of the mandate. For some larger investment banks, this may not be the case.

Local knowledge of funding

Whilst fund raising is not part of a sell side M&A advisor's mandate, a reasonable knowledge of the local acquisition finance market is important, particularly in assessing the ability of prospective purchasers to raise finance in the local market and close the deal.

Access to multi-disciplinary professionals

In addition to being able to offer sound M&A advice, it is often beneficial if one's advisors can offer a 'one stop shop' service. Advisors who have ready access to tax, regulatory, corporate law, competition law, environmental and other relevant professionals can offer a breadth of service which is often not available within a boutique investment bank.

Other advisory services to consider when initiating a sale process

In addition to a lead financial advisor, there are a number of other professional services which may be required in the course of a disposal process:

Financial Due Diligence

Where a Vendor Due Diligence report is to be commissioned (refer to Chapter 6), an accounting firm should be retained to provide Due Diligence services. One consideration here is that where the lead financial advisor is also an accounting firm, you may want to consider an alternative firm as your Due Diligence service provider. Where your lead advisor is incentivised to achieve a successful conclusion of a transaction, there could be a perceived conflict of interest where the same firm is providing a Due Diligence for the benefit of the prospective bidders. Conversely, there is also some merit in using the same firm, as it allows for some synergies between the two teams. Care should be taken though to ensure that bidders' ability to rely on the Vendor Due Diligence is not impaired through concerns they may have over the independence of the Vendor Due Diligence service provider. Due Diligence services may include Financial Due Diligence, Legal Due Diligence, Tax Due Diligence and Environmental Due Diligence.

Data book services

In some cases, an accounting firm may be retained to provide data books. This typically involves the preparation of the majority of the information that would be included in a typical Financial Due Diligence report. But rather than providing independent views and opinions on the target, for the benefit of prospective buyers, limited commentary is provided on numbers. In such cases a conflict would not exist where the same firm preparing data books is the commissioned lead M&A advisor.

Carve Out services

In some cases, especially where a division, which has not previously been accounted for as a separate business unit, is being sold, an accounting form can be commissioned to provide carve out services. A Carve Out aims to prepare a set of financial statements based on a stand-alone business, even if the operation has not previously been accounted for as such.

Property valuer

Where a business is being sold which includes significant properties, especially stand-alone properties, which could be sold separately from the business (For example, commercial property) it may be useful to commission and independent property valuer to perform a valuation of the property.

Tax structuring

Depending on the structure of the seller's organization, or the personal circumstances of the owner, it may be necessary to get some advice on the tax implications of the disposal to the seller.

Virtual Data Room service providers

Almost all transactions require the set-up of a virtual data room. There are several firms who specialize in the hosting of secure virtual data rooms for the controlled sharing of sensitive information for the purposes of facilitating buyer Due Diligence. Key suppliers of these services include Ansarada and Intralinks.

Negotiating advisors terms of reference and fees

Whilst many professional service advisors charge based on estimated time, your lead M&A advisor is normally hired on the basis of some milestone or retainer fees (sometimes also referred to as work fees), with a final success fee. This is generally a preferred basis of charging from the perspective of the seller, as it aligns the interests of the seller with that of their lead M&A advisor. In determining the quantum of the fixed fee milestones, the size of the success fee in relation to the milestone fees is a consideration, with higher fixed fees implying lower success fees and vice versa.

Recent research (Firmex and Divestopedia, 2017) based on a survey of 470 investment bankers and M&A advisors shows the structure of success fees as set out below:

Structure of success fees

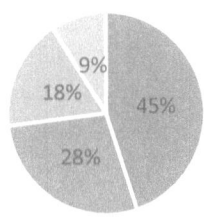

- Scaled percentage
- Simple percentage
- Lehman formula or close varient
- Other

For a scaled percentage structure, a valuation target is set, and a base-level success fee agreed for this valuation, with increments above this target valuation earning successively higher fees. To illustrate, a 50 million dollar target valuation could earn a 2% fee, the next ten million may earn 3%, and any higher valuation 3.5%. The Lehman formula is a descending scale, whereby the first 5 million dollars can be charged at a certain percentage, say 5%, the next five million at another percentage, say3%, and the remaining amount can be charged another percentage, say 2%.

A key consideration in considering the size of the milestone or retainer fees vs the success fee is the likelihood of success. If a business is considered difficult sell by the advisors, or the sellers price expectations are too high, one would typically find that the milestone fees proposed will be higher and the success fees lower. Similarly, for a real juicy mandate with a high probability of closure, one's advisors will be inclined to reduce or even waive any milestone/ retainer fee.

To protect themselves against termination of the contract, advisors will typically insist on a fee tail period clause. This clause requires the seller to pay the success fee regardless of whether the engagement has terminated. It would often only apply if it the business is sold to a party involved in the competitive auction initiated by the advisor, and applies for a stipulated period, generally between 12 and 24 months.

Milestone/ retainer fees would typically include the fees for any deliverables provided by the advisor, including any valuation report and the Information Memorandum, as well as retainer, which is usually charged monthly after completion of the Information Memorandum, and is normally charged for between three and six months. These retainers, are often, but not always, set off the ultimate success fee.

For the purposes of negotiating fees with one's prospective M&A advisors, a seller should first form a view on the attractiveness of the asset and have a sense of the likely valuation. Also, for the purpose of preparing a Request for Proposal, sellers should provide prospective M&A advisors with sufficient information for them to form a view on the likely valuation.

Provided price expectations are not unreasonable, if there is strong interest in the business, this should be factored into the negotiation and pricing of the advisor's fees. Size of the business is also a consideration in deciding who you should be approaching to pitch for the M&A mandate. Smaller/ mid-tier transactions will be of less interest to global investment banks, and should your business have an estimated value of below $10 million, fees charged your big four accounting firms will not be justifiable, in which case local boutiques/ brokers should be considered. Significantly below this level, a properly organised competitive auction process will start to become uneconomical in relation to deal size.

Cultural considerations are also important in negotiating fees. In Anglo-Saxon and western European influenced economies (Europe, North America, Australia, South Africa) there is a greater propensity for retainers and milestone fees, whilst in India and Asia advisors are often forced to accept minimal fixed fees in lieu of higher success fees.

Many large multi-nationals have business development teams, often staffed with ex bankers. Where this is the case, depending on the teams' available capacity, an opportunity exists to limit the time and effort of the sell side advisors. In some of these situations, external M&A advisors are brought in on a time basis to supplement the skills and capacity of the business development team on an ad-hoc basis, where required. However, this does not always work well as the advisors are not immersed in the process and having limited understanding of the process, add less value.

Another factor in negotiating fees, and in deciding on your advisor, is cross border complexity. Any solely domestic transaction is always going to be easier to execute. But where there is cross border, and especially cross cultural transactions, a local boutique will have difficulty executing the mandate efficiently. Here, the focus should be on hiring firms with global reach and teams in the sellers and the targets jurisdiction.

Governance of advisors, communication protocols and approval gates

For the purpose of managing the decision process, and the review and approval of sale documentation, a clear unambiguous approval process should be communicated to the advisor. This may include approval by a steering committee, and ultimately by the board of directors of the seller. Failure to set and communicate appropriate governance and approval protocols, can result in the frustration and/ or delay of the sale process.

Identifying the buyer universe

Broadly, buyers fall into two categories:
- Financial buyers (private equity funds, sovereign wealth funds, High Net Worth family offices, investment trusts, etc.), and
- Strategic or trade buyers.

Financial buyers can further be split between those who manage closed ended funds, which are raised from third party funders (sometimes referred to as limited partners), and financial buyers who invest off their own balance sheets, sometimes referred to as captive funds. Captive funds would include private equity portfolios of banks or other financial institutions. The former typically have a limited investment horizon, linked to the limited duration of their fund, whilst the latter do not have the same restrictions. Funds are often sector and geographically focused in terms of the mandate provided by the limited partner the private equity fund manager (who are often referred to as the general partner). The modus operandi of a typical private equity fund is to generate returns in excess of an agreed hurdle rate, through which they earn an additional incentive fee (referred to as a carried interest). This is done essentially buy buying cheap, providing strategic insight and support through board representation (but not operational involvement) to grow the company, and selling at a higher valuation. To enhance returns, leverage is used as a tool to reduce the initial equity check, and thereby enhance the returns to the financial buyer. Private equity firms typically back management and seek to partner with the management team by ensuring they are joint investors in the business.

As a seller, one should appreciate that other than providing optimal financing structures, private equity firms typically do not benefit from strategic and operational synergies which may be available to a trade buyer. In addition, a low purchase price is important for private equity firms to achieve their incentives. Accordingly, where there is clear interest from trade buyers, a private equity buyer is unlikely to be able to offer a competitive price.

The circumstances where one should consider private equity buyers would include situations where the business cannot be sold to the obvious trade buyer because of anti-trust considerations, or where there are no obvious clear trade buyer who would benefit from any synergies. Another situation could be where the shareholders amongst themselves would like to facilitate the transfer of ownership between an owner/ manager and the next generation of management. As private equity deals are normally funded with a significant proportion of debt, the business in question should be generating reasonable cash flows to be able to support acquisition finance being raised from banks.

When considering a buyer list, a key consideration is the stake for sale. Typically, strategic buyers would insist on a majority stake, and therefore a sale of a minority stake would limit the buyer list (unless a clear route to a majority stake is provided). In some cases, for strategic and or political situations – and in certain countries this is regulated through statute - the inclusion of a local partner into a business is required. In these situations, a different type of buyer is sought.

Strategic buyers can be competitors, suppliers and/ or customers. They could be local, i.e. from within the country of the target, or they could be a global competitor looking to enter the market.

Usually, as part of any respectable sell side investment bank pitch, a number of prospective buyers will be identified. The process where you request proposals, is therefore a useful tool to identify prospective buyers. However, this should be augmented by further research, and often management will have some ideas of their own around potential buyers. Sometimes owners of a business would have already been approached by parties, and often line management will themselves have an idea about likely buyers. If your advisors are a global investment bank, or accounting/ advisory firm, they should have access to international sector experts, and it is useful for them to reach out to their internal network of M&A bankers to get global buyer ideas.

In order to facilitate a process of selection of a list of prospective buyers, the preparation of a long list is sometimes useful, with a tearing of prospective bidders according to the seller's requirements. This can then be discussed and debated, following which a short list of bidders to approach can be put together.

Determining the length of the buyer list

Whilst the process described in this book can theoretically be run with a single buyer, its key benefit is that it is designed to accommodate multiple buyer, to increase the certainty of concluding a transaction and maximizing price for the seller.

The exact number of parties to make initial contact with is a matter for discussion with your advisors. The experience of the author is that the desire for confidentiality is a key determinant of the size and extent of the buyer list. In addition, buyer lists where international buyers are sought are considerably longer than for transactions focusing on domestic buyers.

The author has managed contact programs for buyer lists approaching 100 participants, although the typical number of parties to contact would be between 10 and 30.

Often the list of prospective buyers is split into categories or tiers, with more likely buyers being contacted first (second and third tier buyers can be considered based on initial feedback from first tier buyers).

Involving private equity firms in a competitive auction process

A critical component of any private equity funds' investment decision is partnering with management as investors in a business. Therefore, involving private equity firms in a competitive auction process creates complexity and a significant conflict of interest for the management team, which needs to be carefully managed by the seller and their advisors.

A competitive auction process is designed to allow limited management interaction, particularly during the phase of the disposal process where non-binding offers are solicited. In any successful disposal process, the management are key to maximizing the selling price. In a situation where a private equity firm is invited into a competitive process, they may try to circumvent the planned auction process, as co-operation and alignment with management is a key premise under which they will invest.

Particular care should therefore be taken to get management to commit to the competitive auction process and not to engage directly with the bidders during the non-binding offer phase of the sale process. Direct contact between a private equity bidder, and management, may unduly influence management. However, it is also important to acknowledge that for any private equity transaction partnering with the management team is critical, and for a private equity firm to arrive at any meaningful offer they will need to engage with management and formulate an ownership structure which includes the management team.

When including private equity in a bidding process, one should prohibit contact between the bidder and the management team during the non-binding offer phase. During the Due Diligence phase one could then allow the private equity buyer the opportunity for some alone time with the management team, usually after the management presentation. One can request an up-front agenda for this meeting. There should be a very clear message to the management team and the private equity bidder that there can be no discussion around pricing of competitor bids. Clearly this approach will require a certain degree of trust between the seller and the target management team. Discussions in these private equity/ management sessions should be limited to management's capacity and appetite to participate in the management buyout.

Once there is in principle agreement, then the completion of a shareholders' agreement can be retained as a suspensive condition in any mark-up of the final offer Sale and Purchase Agreement. Alternatively the key terms of any shareholders agreement should be included with the final offer, and these can be shared by the sell side M&A advisor with the management team during the assessment/ review of final offers received.

Preparing forecasts

Typically, when preparing a business for sale, forecast information is provided to prospective bidders, usually for at least three years, but often for five years. Forecasts are normally subject to detailed scrutiny during Due Diligence, so it is important that they are robustly prepared. The forecasts should talk to other strategy documents and business plans that are prepared for the company, as these are likely to be scrutinized during Due Diligence for consistency. Where three-year forecasts are prepared as part of a standard budgeting process, care should be taken not to diverge from these forecasts without due cause, as these budgeting forecasts are likely to be accessed by the bidders during Due Diligence.

It is important that they include some of the future prospects, however they should not be overly optimistic, as management's buy in to their achievement is critical. Advisors can be useful to test and probe management on the forecasts, as they will have the ability to introduce the scepticism that other professionals will have during the interrogation of forecasts in the Due Diligence process. It is important for the seller to support the advisor in getting to a position whereby you have optimistic, yet justifiable forecasts. It is counter-productive when forecasts are subsequently discredited by bidders during the Due Diligence process.

In addition to the forecast plan, one would typically also need to identify positive prospects which are not in the plan, either because they are premature, or because they are difficult to accurately quantify.

Before finalizing any forecasts, they should be subject to a Discounted Cash Flow (DCF) valuation to ensure that the resultant value is in line with the sellers' expectations (refer to chapter 4).

CASE STUDY: Management bias in Forecasts

In author was appointed by a multi-national client to sell their South African subsidiary. As part of the planning phase of the sale process, the advisors, together with the overseas seller engaged with the management to prepare forecasts. The business had a particularly strong-willed and dynamic CEO who had lead the company for many years.

The advisors objective in preparing a three-year business plan was to present a position that represented an optimistic, but achievable set of forecasts. Through a detailed process of discussion and enquiry, which included a detailed review of existing long-term contracts and expected contracts, we were able to agree a position we expected management would defend.

Having agreed the forecasts, and prepared the Information Memorandum, the advisors went to market to find prospective buyers. Three prospective buyers submitted non-binding offers, and it emerged that the leading buyer was a private equity firm. Through this process, the CEO become an equity partner with the private equity firm. Because of this the CEO took the critique the forecasts, advising his prospective partners where there were risks to the achievement of the forecasts. To make matters worse, the operations of the business had been affected by a downturn in the market and operational issues which impacted the achievability of the forecasts.

Ultimately the business was sold – albeit at a value lower than was supported by the forecasts. As the CEO was key to the successful sale, he was able to negotiate favorable terms for himself.

This case study serves to illustrate the importance and role of management in buying into and supporting forecast financial information. It also illustrates the risks associated with involving a private equity firm in a competitive sale process, and the conflict of interest between management and the seller when executing a sale to a private equity buyer.

Normalising historical results

When considering historical results, it is important to consider whether any adjustment may be required to the historical financial statements.

It is also important to consider the format of the historical information presented. This is driven by the requirements for a valuation, key being the breakdown of key line items to arrive at Earnings Before Interest, Tax, Depreciation and Amortization, working capital changes, and capital expenditure.

Often, particularly in owner managed businesses, there are certain expenses which would not continue when the business is separately owned. Examples could include excessive salaries for the owner manager or rental which is not market related. These should be explained and adjusted in the forecasts which are presented to prospective bidders. Often in corporate owned businesses there are excessive head office charges, including management fees. These would not be relevant on a stand-alone basis and should also be adjusted.

In addition to adjusting for the above, there may be certain once-off items of income and expense which are not recurring and distort the historical trends. This could include a once-off large legal claim, or a particularly large non-recurring windfall revenue item. These should be identified, and consideration given to separately disclosing and/ or adjusting these in the forecast.

Critical to maximizing value, is being able to present a positive historic trend showing consistent and stable earnings growth. If the adjustments above can achieve this, it would be recommended that you adjust for the purpose of presenting the historic financial information.

Whilst a key valuation methodology is the DCF based on forecast earnings, greater reliance is always placed on the DCF if it is underpinned by historic earnings which support the trends feeding into the growth assumptions in the business plan.

Carve out considerations

When selling a part of a business, for example a division, care needs to be taken to appropriately prepare the forecasts for the purpose of presenting to prospective bidders. A division is normally supported by central/ head office support functions such as Information Technology, Human Resources and Finance. An estimate should be made of what these costs might be, if the business were independent. This will be important for any financial buyer. However, when selling to a trade buyer, one should rather focus on the cash flows and earning which can be added *before* any central/ head office costs, as many of these central/ head office costs may not be duplicated in the buyers organization.

Often the most value is derived if the target can be supported by the pre-existing support services/ infrastructure of the acquirer. In this case, the valuation will then exclude the negative effect of any central costs. Whilst the seller will seek to capture some of these synergistic benefits, through the competitive bidding process, it may equally create stranded costs through excess capacity at the head office of the seller. This will be a drain on value for the company going forward.

4. Valuation

Why do a valuation, the reverse test?

In preparing for a business disposal, one is often led to question the benefit of preparing a valuation. The nature of the process is designed to solicit the best offer, so why bother with your own valuation? The old adage, that beauty is in the eye of the beholder, is most appropriate for a competitive auction process. The valuation is driven by the competitive tension and the respective views of each buyer, as well as the terms of negotiated warranties and indemnities. What a seller and their advisors see as fair value of a business is hardly of any relevance to a buyer and their investment decisions.

Notwithstanding, preparing a valuation provides benefit to the seller. In particular a valuation serves to confirm that forecast information provided supports the seller's valuation expectation. The most common valuation techniques are forward looking and usually based on cash flows to the business owner. Accordingly, the valuation is a useful 'reverse test' to assess the forecasts prepared by management. A sellers' primary objective in a sale process is usually to maximize value, and it is therefore plain to see, that a defendable, but optimistic forecast, will maximize value to the seller, to the extent that the achievability can be sold (or better, warranted – refer page 62) to the buyer.

Of course, different buyers will have different views on valuation. A key part of any valuation is likely to be synergies, so in addition to a stand-alone valuation based on the business as-is, a seller may want to consider what likely costs savings may accrue to the prospective buyers. A valuation including an assessment of synergistic benefits is likely to result in a ceiling price, above the stand-alone valuation, and a value to be accrued as a result of benefits being introduced by the buyer. Buyers will be loath to pass these on to the seller, but a well-run competitive auction will likely result in a significant proportion of this synergistic value being accrued to the seller.

CASE STUDY: Synergies in a Valuation

In the mid 2000's, the author was called in to assist the business development team of a large bank on the sale of their internet service provider business. In the mid-nineties the bank had introduced free email accounts for all banking customers. This was based on the then prevalent 'dial up' technology. The bank saw the future of banking as being dominated by on line services and felt that by offering a free dial up service to support their internet banking service, they could attract significant new customers. This rapidly undercut other dial up internet service providers in the market as many new customers opened bank accounts to receive the free internet service.

Whilst the numbers of sign-ons were initially impressive, the internet services division of the bank never achieved significant profitability, despite the subsequent introduction of moderate fees for internet services. In the early years of the 2000's dial-up services began to be replaced by ADSL. This made the service offering less attractive. Further, due to the regulatory burden of operating a large complex financial institution, the back office of the banks internet services division was much more expensive that could be offered elsewhere. Given that the bank could redeploy these people elsewhere in the organization, it was felt that a significantly higher level of profitability could be achieved if the business was owned by an internet services company. The standalone profits and future cash flows of the business, based on management prepared forecasts on an as-is basis reflected a business in terminal decline, with a DCF valuation of close to nothing.

Through discussion and enquiry, the advisor was able to prepare forecast based on a more realistic costs structure of a competitor. This included a nimbler back office with lower costs to support the business. This reflected a much more favorable valuation. However, the real value on the business, which was not evident to the bank, was actually in the value of the customers who would likely convert to an ADSL when purchased by a competing internet services provider.

Ultimately the buyer (an established internet services provider) paid multiples of the banks' initial valuation expectation. Whilst this was partly due to cost synergies that could be achieved, the real premium came in through the future value which would only be available to an ADSL service provider who could easily migrate these customers to a higher yielding ADSL service offering.

This case study highlights:
- *The benefits of considering synergies in a valuation (and ensuring this story is succinctly communicated to the buyer);*
- *The benefits of considering buyers who would see strategic upside beyond what is available to the seller, and finally;*

- *The benefit of the competitive sale process, which allows for some of the synergistic value to accrue to the seller.*

Whilst the valuation was never provided to the seller, this process did allow for the seller to 'discover' the hot spots to increase the price. It also ensured that the correct buyers were targeted and that the forecasts supported a higher bidding price.

Basis of valuation

Discounted cash flow

A Discounted Cash Flow (DCF), based of forecast free cash flows accruing to the owner of a business, is the most common methodology for valuing a business. This method involves discounting future cash flows at the Weighted Average Cost of Capital (WACC). In determining the WACC, consideration should be given to the nature of the prospective buyer. Whilst a standalone business might have a higher discount rate, for the purpose of evaluating a disposal, one should consider the likely buyer universe and the likely funding thereof, to determine the value to the prospective buyer.

Comparable multiples (traded and implied by transactions)

In addition to a DCF valuation, one should consider comparable traded multiples of historic earnings for similar listed companies (where appropriate comparators are available), and recent earnings multiples implied by similar transactions in the market. In evaluating earnings multiples, use is frequently made of Earnings Before Interest, Depreciation and Amortization (EBITDA) as this eliminates the distorting effect of differing amounts of debt amongst comparators. An EBITDA multiple valuation determines the enterprise value of a business before the deduction of interest on debt.

Investment decision making by buyers who are public listed companies, are in particular driven by their own traded multiples, as these are usually under scrutiny by their shareholders, and the broader investment community. Depending on the size of the transaction, the regulators may require listed companies to publish the pro-forma financial effects of the transaction, so being able to add earnings to their income statement at a cost less than their own earnings (being measured through their traded multiples) becomes an important consideration in justifying the acquisition to shareholders.

Buy out metrics

Private equity buyers, who are incentivized based on carried interest fees earned above benchmarks, will typically run a buy-out model, interposing the anticipated debt into the business to forecast the expected Internal Rate of Return (IRR) generated for their fund. Where bidders are expected to be financial buyer/ private equity buyers, it is a good idea to run an MBO model, interposing expected acquisition finance and management participation. IRR's hurdles for private equity buyers are generally 20 - 25%, depending on currency of the fund, so one can figure out the likely valuation implied by a five-year MBO model.

Over time there has been a correlation between both interest rates, level of acquisition debt provided in the market (usually measured as a multiple of the targets historical EBITDA) and the valuations being paid by financial buyers. These should form part of the expectations of any seller targeting a sale to a financial buyer.

Premiums and discounts to valuation

When considering a DCF valuation, one's WACC is always derived from public sources, with the starting point being observable market data. In arriving at an appropriate company specific WACC one does need to consider adjustments to reflect company specific considerations. In addition to determining the appropriate WACC, comparable multiple valuations also need to be adjusted to reflect company specific matters which would need to be taken into account as an adjustment to multiples implied by observable market data.

Control premia

A factor which will have an impact on the valuation is the stake of the business being sold, with a majority/ controlling stake attracting a premium relative to a minority stake, so this should be considered in arriving at any valuation. A DCF valuation and transaction M&A multiple is generally considered a majority valuation, whilst traded multiples of listed companies being considered a minority valuation. Research performed by PwC in South Africa (based on averages for respondents to a valuation survey) suggests the average control premium applied to the market value of equity is 16% for an interest in the range of 51% – 74% and 21% in the range 75% – 100%. Where joint control exists, respondents indicated that they applied a control premium of 8% on average. (PwC, 2017)

Marketability adjustments

Marketability discounts can be defined as 'the ability to convert the business ownership interest to cash quickly, with minimum transaction and administrative costs in so doing and with a high degree of certainty of realizing the expected amount of net proceeds. (Pratt, 2000)

A critical factor in assessing the discount would be if a company is listed, and if it is, the liquidity of the stock relative to peer companies. Another which affect the size of the discount include the size of the stake in the business being valued, with a controlling interest typically attracting a lower discount as it would be easier to sell.

Discounts to vary according to region. In South Africa, research by PwC suggests that discounts applied by valuation practitioners range between 7% and 10% for controlling interest but could be as high as 20% for minority stakes. (PwC, 2017)

Small stock premiums

To adjust for the increased risk of a small stock, relative to a comparator group that represents large stocks, a discount is normally applied. This will be applied based on judgement and also based on the size of the company relative to the comparator group. Typically, this discount would be in the region of 10% to 20% but may also be influenced by the factors below.

The property decision

Where a business has significant properties, the valuation, and the sales process may need to be amended. Where properties form part of a company, but are easily marketable and saleable, separately from the business, one should consider carving out this value from the business value. Assuming properties are not bespoke to a particular business enterprise, and therefore separable, they are considered by investors to be of lower risk than a business.

Accordingly, they typically attract a lower discount rate to the future cash flows than businesses cash flows. Whilst a business may attract be valued based on a WACC 15% or more, a property would generally be expected to yield a net rental income of less than 10%. Said differently, relative to a business, properties generally trade at a higher multiple of the earnings they generate. Therefore, valuing the property separately – and marketing it separately in a sale process - the will generally attract a higher valuation based on the rental yield, than would be generated through higher cash flows in a business without a rental charge. Accordingly marketing the properties separately is often advisable.

Therefore, it may be better to produce cash flows of a property-owning business, on a pro-forma basis after deduction notional market related rental, for the property and then valuing the property separately. Similarly, when initiating a disposal of the business, it is often advisable to request bidders to pitch separately for the business and the property. If the property value offered by bidders is inadequate, the seller may look to retain the property and lease it to the tenant or sell the property to a specialist property investor who would likely pay a fairer price for the property.

When to do the valuation

Whilst a business valuation is of interest to a seller in setting price expectations, a more important objective is to assess the implications of the forecast. Accordingly, the valuation should be completed during the planning phase. In addition, ones advisor's remuneration is usually linked to the achievement of value, sometimes with an incentive kicker if the expected valuation is exceeded. It is therefore important for a seller to determine the value of the business prior to negotiating as fee with ones lead M&A advisor. It is equally only fair that one provides reasonable historic and forecast information to one's advisors before they arrive at a proposed fee. Whilst a valuation is usually part of an M&A mandate, it would be inappropriate for the seller not to have at least formulated an initial view on valuation prior to signing on an advisor. Sometimes there is further merit in agreeing to revisit the success fee percentage once the initial valuation is prepared by the advisor. It is plain to see, though, that the incentive will always be for ones advisor to understate the value of a business where it forms part of the negotiation of his fees.

Stranded costs

When a large corporate looks at selling a division, care needs to be taken in considering the financial impact of what is left behind. Sometimes referred to as a negative synergy, the sale of a division may often result in certain allocated costs having to be picked up by other divisions in the group, through the reallocation of overheads. This may include group insurance costs, finance, HR and IT costs. The sale of a business may not result in any savings in these areas, which would result in these costs having to be subsumed by the group (whereas they were previously charged to the division). In evaluating any disposal, the effect of these costs on the remaining groups needs to be considered in order to establish a holistic picture of the financial and valuation implications of the transaction on the broader enterprise.

Financial services businesses valuation

Typically, when valuing a financial services business such as a bank or an insurance company, Return on Equity (ROE) is an important factor, and one that is critical for a financial services buyer in assessing the attractiveness of an acquisition. Unlike manufacturing businesses and those with plant and other fixed assets, the Net Asset Value (NAV) of a bank generally approximates the fair value of its assets, and therefore, the ROE equates to the return on capital invested.

Therefore, when considering the value, an important analysis is the valuation implied by comparable ROE's for traded listed financial services companies, after adjusting for company specific risks.

When considering an earnings-based valuation, care should be taken to adjust cash flows, for additional capital required to be retained to safely comply with the regulatory capital requirements to meet current and forecasts business levels.

For this reason, the income approach to valuation needs to be modified from a traditional discounting of free cash flows to all providers of capital (debt and equity), to the discounting of free cash flows available to equity providers. The methodology called the Free Cash flow to Equity Approach, or an approach which discounts dividends at the Cost of Equity (rather than the cost of debt) will generally be used to value banks and insurance companies.

5. Marketing documentation for the indicative offer phase

The nature, timing and extent of the documentation to be prepared for a competitive auction sale process is driven by the nature process. There is a progressive disclosure of further information to bidders as they move through the process. Initially a one to two page anonymous 'teaser' can be issued to pique interest, followed by an Information Memorandum, which includes more detail to allow a party to assess value and formulate a Non-binding Indicative Offer. Ultimately shortlisted parties are invited to participate in a Due Diligence which allows for meetings with management, site visits and access to a comprehensive data room containing significant corporate information and documentation.

The non-disclosure agreement

As a first step in any process, before one makes contact with potential bidders, one should prepare a Non-Disclosure Agreement (NDA), sometimes also referred to as a confidentiality agreement.

In his entire professional career, the author never been involved in any process where any legal action has resulted from the breach of a NDA. Having said that, the author has often experienced leakages from bidders. Whilst these experiences may call in to question the efficacy of an NDA, the author is firmly of the view that it is still a critical document to protect not only the seller, but also importantly, the business being sold. Whilst the process of negotiating of NDAs can be a frustration to bidders, it is worth highlighting to them, that should they become the ultimate owners of the business, they would have wanted the business they ultimately own, to be protected from all other unsuccessful bidders in the process.

Thus, the process of negotiating and executing an NDA is a useful tool to focus the mind of the bidder, and bind them, even if just ethically, to maintain confidentiality. I expect without NDAs in place, leakages of information would be substantially more frequent.

From the authors' experience in negotiating NDAs, the following are some of the important clauses:

Time/ duration

NDAs should have a time limit as it is unreasonable for a bidder to sign an NDA in perpetuity. Furthermore, information provided through the M&A process becomes less sensitive through the passage of time and disclosure thereof should, therefore be acceptable to the seller. A five-year term is often a starting point for sellers, although a three year term would be a satisfactory compromise. The author has seen two years and even 18 months agreed, but this duration starts to compromise the seller and the target business, especially considering that the time to negotiate and conclude a deal to the execution of a Sale and Purchase Agreement (SPA) can often take 12 months or longer. Another consideration could be to add an additional term stipulating that the duration of the NDA extends for a pre-determined period commencing from the termination of negotiations between the parties.

Jurisdiction

Where dealing in cross border transactions, foreign buyers will often resist a non-disclosure agreement governed in accordance with the laws of the local jurisdiction, preferring to be able to defend their rights through the courts in their home jurisdiction. This might not be acceptable to the seller (depending on the jurisdiction of the buyer is trying to impose on the seller) and as a compromise, the seller may suggest a neutral jurisdiction that both seller and bidder are comfortable with (the United Kingdom is often used).

Non-solicitation of employees, and contact with management

As a seller, it is important that bidders agree not to make contact with any of the sellers' management, without the consent and agreement of the seller or their advisors. A competitive auction process is, by its nature, disruptive to a business, often resulting in the management taking their eye off the ball. In order to minimize this, bidders must agree to comply with the rules of the game, by agreeing not to make contact, especially during the indicative offer phase. During the later Due Diligence phase, contact can be provided, but this should be managed through the sellers' advisors. In addition to maintaining control of the process, and limiting unnecessary contact with management, one should also insist on (especially in respect of strategic/ trade buyers) a non-solicitation clause, whereby bidders agree not to solicit the targets staff for employment. This is an obvious protection to ensure that the sellers' business is not damaged as a result of a failed auction process. The author has seen situations, where the management of a company has been poached after the buyer realized that the best asset of the business was the management which could be purchased at a lower cost than the business.

Carve outs for release of information

Whilst the preference of any seller would be to limit any and all disclosure of information, it is reasonable for the bidder to insist that it comply with any legal and/ or regulatory commitment it may have to release information.

Appropriate use of information

Clearly the huge risk for any seller in dealing with a competitor is that sensitive market information is used not to evaluate the business, but for the bidders own strategic value. Accordingly, an important clause is one requiring that the information provided may only be used specifically for the evaluation of the investment opportunity. Further, a clause requiring that unsuccessful bidders return and/ or destroy all confidential information is critical. Whilst these clauses are often included, the author is always surprised at how often this request is not followed up on by advisors. As a matter of course, the author is of the view that all bidders who withdraw from a process, or whom with the seller terminates discussions, should be requested to confirm in writing that they have returned and/or destroyed all information. Whilst there is no way to police this, in this day and age, the author believes the request in itself focusses the mind of the bidder and is an important tool to protect the target company's valuable and sensitive strategic commercial information, particularly when dealing with strategic bidders who are potential competitors.

Clause on non-disclosure of bids

Whilst the primary purpose of the NDA is to protect the seller and the target business, it is reasonable for the bidder to insist that the NDA works both ways. Whilst the seller does not typically disclose sensitive information about itself, disclosure of the terms of any bidders offer can obviously be detrimental to the bidder. It is therefore not unreasonable for a bidder to request that the seller (and its advisors) undertake not to disclose any details of its offer, or even the fact that they participating in the sale process.

Negotiating changes to an NDA

Some bidders will simply sign and return an NDA without mark-ups. However, others, particularly larger and more professionally run organizations, will pass on an NDA to their internal legal team, who will no doubt have comments they may wish to negotiate with the seller. This can be a particularly administratively burdensome process for any seller. It is therefore advisable for the seller to identify someone from their internal legal team (or their external legal advisors) to assist the M&A advisors in the negotiation of the NDA. Often the same routine queries come up from bidders, such as jurisdiction, duration of agreement, etc. Where the seller is comfortable, they can provide a mandate to their advisors to negotiate some of these points to an acceptable level. For example, the duration of the draft NDA provided could stipulate a duration of 5 years, whilst agreeing up front that an acceptable compromise might be 3 years.

Clean team NDA

In a time of increased regulatory scrutiny and with the advent of anti-trust laws, it is sometimes necessary for the seller to provide further data room access for certain members of the buyers deal teams. This would be the case where the buyer is a competitor to the target business. Under these situations, it may be necessary that certain information on the target company that could be strategically valuable to bidders, cannot be shared with line management at the acquirer, but only within the deal team (who are not involved in managing the bidders' day to day operations). This does complicate the management of the virtual data room and may require an additional clean room only accessible by approved 'clean team' members. In these situations, an ancillary/supplementary clean team NDA may need to be signed to further restrict the information in the clean room.

The Teaser

Before sharing an Information Memorandum, it is important that prospective bidders sign the NDA. In order to first determine their interest participating in any sale process, bidders will need to understand the nature of the opportunity. In order to describe the opportunity, a confidential investment overview, would normally be prepared. This is often aptly referred to as a 'teaser'. An alternative, if the seller does not want any documentation to go out before the signing of an NDA, is for the seller and their advisors agree on a script, which would allow the advisor to explain the opportunity verbally, to determine prospective bidders' interest. A teaser, which is shared with the recipient prior to binding them to a confidentiality agreement, typically does not disclose the name of the business. To maintain confidentiality a project name is typically used. Included in the teaser is the geographic location of the business, the sector, key clients, revenue and possibly EBITDA. Some historical trends, and forecasts in relation to financial information, may be added. Also included is the contact details of the advisors. Typically, the teaser is distributed with the NDA to prospective bidders. It is essential that the sellers' advisor and the seller agree exactly who is being contacted during this process. In certain instances, preliminary contact may have been made between some bidders and the seller, in which case the seller may want to make initial contact with the bidder, but thereafter to ensure proper management and co-ordination of the process, further contact should be maintained only by the seller's advisors.

In some cases, a script is prepared in conjunction with a Teaser. This is useful where it is believed that a greater impact can be made through a conversation, rather than an email. In a globally marketed disposal process, a script is even more important as in these circumstances it is likely the seller's advisors will be using their global network to reach out to bidders, and the advisors employee making contact with the foreign bidder may not be familiar with the target business.

The Information Memorandum

Purpose of an Information Memorandum

An Information Memorandum forms the principle marketing document during the Non-Binding Indicative Offer phase of the disposal process. It is typically co-branded with the logo of the advisor who is typically responsible for preparing the document.

The Information Memorandum is generally distributed to a wide audience of prospective bidders. The objective of the document is to provide sufficient information as to allow a prospective bidder to arrive at a valuation for the purpose of submitting a Non-binding Indicative Offer (which would still be subject to Due Diligence). As such, the information memorandum should have sufficient information for a reasonable buyer to make an assessment of the business, without the need for access to management or further information. The author has been involved in processes where in excess of sixty parties have been approached with teasers. In some cases, it may be significantly less, but the main purpose of an Information Memorandum always remains the same; to facilitate a desk-top assessment of the business, without site access and management interaction. It is therefore important to ensure a well-constructed document is prepared with all critical information included.

An overview of the key components of an Information Memorandum follows.

The rationale for the disposal

A question always asked by prospective bidders is: "why sell?" Often a reason for selling a business is under performance or concerns over the long term future of a business. This is generally not an attractive proposition for a prospective buyer and should be avoided.

A disposal rationale which does not reflect negatively on the business is better received, provided the seller can pitch a convincing rationale which speaks to the interests of the buyer. Examples of these reasons include, change in strategic direction at head office, succession limitations in an owner managed business, or for a financial buyer, an end of fund life requiring a sale in terms of the fund mandate.

Another attractive reason for a sale is that the business is constrained by the current owner (for example for regulatory reasons) and that the business prospects will be significantly better in the hands of a new owner.

The rationale for disposal therefore also links into the equity story, which should speak to the anticipated target buyer audience. Where it is anticipated that an aspect of the business will be attractive to particular buyers, this should clearly be accentuated in the Information Memorandum, even where this may not be part of management's prevailing strategy.

Generally, the rationale for the disposal is included in the body of the Information Memorandum, however there may be circumstances that the seller may want to tailor the message for the particular audience. In addition to a standard, generic Information Memorandum, the Information Memorandum is accompanied by a covering letter, often referred to as a 'Process Letter'. This letter is customized for the particular bidder. Where there are particular benefits or synergies which relate to a particular buyer, and the seller wants to communicate this separately to unique buyers, then the sales rationale can be excluded from the Information Memorandum and included in the Process Letter. The Process Letter is further discussed in chapter 7.

Country and market overview

When contacting bidders globally, it is useful to give an overview of the country, or countries of operation, including basic macroeconomic information. This information is generally public and readily available but is nevertheless useful to include in the same document to facilitate the bidders' learning curve. A further benefit is that local bidders can appreciate that international bidders are looking at the opportunity, thereby increasing the competitive tension. The author has even seen market information being included with the specific objective of sending this message to local buyers.

Drilling down into the competitive landscape is also important. Whilst local trade buyers, particularly if they are competitors, will generally have an appreciation of the market, financial buyers and international bidders may be less familiar with the market. The advisor should have access to information sources, but also the target management should have a good understanding of their competitive environment and the market tends/ dynamics.

Care should be taken in presenting market dynamics where bidders are likely to be competitors, and it may be advisable to consult with a competition lawyer to ensure it is appropriate to share market information with competitors.

Management and Human resources

In reviewing the Information Memorandum, the bidders generally won't have access to management. It is therefore important to include a brief profile of each of the key management of the business. This would typically include as a minimum the CEO, CFO, and key divisional heads. An organogram should be included to give a sense of the organizational structure, together with staff numbers, standard terms of employment, total payroll cost, union information, etc.

Suppliers, customers

Subject to the need to maintain confidentiality (refer to Redacting information in an Information Memorandum, page 68), details of suppliers and customers, including market share should be included.

Where a business reports divisional results separately, the narrative around customers, suppliers and markets should mirror this with a separate overview of each division.

Processes

Particularly in a manufacturing environment, manufacturing processes, manufacturing capacity, and details of plant and machinery can be key considerations for prospective buyers. Details of plant (including pictures) can be provided to assist the prospective bidders in their assessment.

In addition to the above, details of the operations and infrastructure of the business should be provided, including Marketing and Communication, Information Technology, Human Resources, Finance, Legal and Compliance.

Financial results and forecasts

For the purpose of arriving at a valuation, it is obviously key that historical financial results and forecasts are provided. This should include forecast working capital and capital expenditure as this is important to arrive at a valuation. Either a forecast balance sheet should be provided, or a basis for determining net working capital. Preparing forecasts on page 32, provides guidance on preparing forecasts for a disposal process.

Forecasts often form the basis for discussions and negotiations around price. Depending on a seller's confidence around the forecasts, a seller may want to consider offering a profit warranty. Particularly in the sale of an owner managed business, management are often expected to stay on for a period, typically a year post transaction. In these situations, a tool to maximize value, if the seller is comfortable, is to offer to warrant the forecast profits, typically the first years profits post transaction.

This may be stated in the Information Memorandum, or in the covering Process Letter. Where a profit warranty is offered, it can provide incremental comfort to bidders and result in them pitching their non-binding offer at a higher price than would otherwise be the case.

Property

A decision needs to be made as to whether owned property or property owned by related parties (e.g. a shareholder) should be included as part of the sale package. To a large extent this depends on whether the property is unique to the business of the target (such as a farm, or a specialized manufacturing facility), or could be sold as a stand-alone property (such as the commercial office building, or a retail premises). Whilst a unique/ bespoke property should always be included as part of the sale package, there is some flexibility with regard to other property. In Chapter 7 we deal with how to present the sale assets as an optional package which can be selected based on bidder preferences (see specifically page 87).

Assuming the property is to be sold, details (including photographs) should all included in order for the buyer to arrive at a valuation. Other information should include location, size (total property and under roof), usage (commercial vs warehouse) management costs, utilities, fair market rental, etc.

It is fairly common in an owner managed business that the property is owned by a separate entity owned by the same owners of the business being sold. Often the rental charges for the business premises is not market related. For example, it could be set at a level linked to the mortgage payments, which in cases could be higher than the market related rental, or the rental change could be driven by tax planning considerations. In these situations, it is important to give due consideration to what a market related lease should be. The Information Memorandum should clearly stipulate what the market related rental is and make pro-forma adjustments to the historical and forecast financial information to reflect the true profitability of the business bringing in a market related rental expense.

Beyond the plan

A careful balance needs to be struck between disclosing an overly optimistic outlook and being too cautious in preparing forecasts. Clearly, forecast need to have the buy in of management and be defendable under scrutiny, which will become acute during the Due Diligence phase of the sale process, when advisors typically hire external advisors to perform a Due Diligence review.

There will typically be an expectation that an optimistic view will be taken of the forecasts by sellers, and a skeptical approach will likely be taken by any bidder. It can therefore be counterproductive to prepare forecasts which are overly conservative.

Often a business will have positive and negative factors which may have a bearing on the future prospects of the business but are not included in the business plans. These may include the effect of a potential new contract, the impact of new regulations, or anticipated market trends. They may not be included in any financial forecasts because the probability of an extraneous event is difficult to estimate, or because management in unable to quantify the effect thereof. Where positive, it is important that these factors are included in the Information Memorandum, highlighting that the effect is not in the forecasts, and where possible providing a quantification of the potential impact. Any investment/ cost associated with the strategy needs to be clearly set out. Inclusion of these upside factors are important to drive up the price during the bidding process.

Events that are negative should not be ignored, as these factors are likely to emerge during the Due Diligence process. They should therefore be disclosed together with management's plans to mitigate the events. Sometimes these factors are included in the information memorandum as part of a SWOT analysis.

CASE STUDY: Non-disclose negative information in Information Memorandum, presentation of key synergies

The author was hired to advise on the sale of a private equity owned pan African services business, headquartered in South Africa with operations in 15 African countries. Whilst on the face of it the business appeared to be reasonably diverse, with strong earnings growth prospects in an attractive market, close scrutiny revealed that there was a significant reliance on one key customer who accounted for about 40% of revenue, but around 60% of the EBITDA margin. The customer was a notoriously difficult client, and there had been some historic disputes in relation to the account.

The key bidder emerged as another private equity owned competitor, bidding an attractive multiple of 7 x EBITDA in the Non-binding Indicative Offer Phase. The Information Memorandum did not reveal the extent of reliance on the customer, but during due diligence it did emerge. The final bidders offer was accordingly reduced significantly, offering the same multiple for the rest of the business and a significantly reduced multiple for the EBITDA linked to the key customer contract. Ultimately the buyer and seller could not agree on the valuation, and the bidder walked away.

A key learning from this process was the impact that a key unidentified risk can have on a bidder when it emerges through due diligence. Usually it can be advisable to flag risks – and mitigations – upfront in the Information Memorandum. During the competitive auction phase, when bidding competition is greater, a bidder will discount the offer less than when he has achieved preferred bidder status.

Shortly thereafter the key customer terminated the contract with the company, resulting in significantly reduced earnings.

Five years later, following efforts to rebuild the revenue base, the author was again approached to recommence the process. This time it was identified that a key differentiator was the potential cost savings to competitors, which could result if the head office was significantly curtailed. This proved a difficult to illustrate in the Information Memorandum, but a careful presentation of EBITDA before and after head office costs with a breakdown of head office costs, proved key to illustrating the costs structure of the business to the bidder, and provided each bidder with the information required to evaluate the potential cost saving that could result from a head office restructuring.

A sale agreement was eventually signed with a different competitor, which was active in a number of other competing countries.[1]

---

[1] Ultimately the sale got bogged down in a complex anti-trust approval process in

Synergies

It is sometimes the case that there will be synergistic benefits that may be derived by certain bidders. When preparing the Information Memorandum, it is therefore important to provide the information necessary for the prospective bidder to assess the likely cost savings or revenue enhancement opportunities.

Sometimes these may be very sensitive, and the approach to disclosing needs to be carefully considered. For example, there may be head office costs that can be eliminated by some potential trade buyers. This is clearly something you would not want to highlight to management (bearing in mind that management is the principle contact you have during the preparation of the Information Memorandum). Clearly setting out the head office costs with sufficient detail to allow the bidder to assess the composition of the head office cost, together with likely savings needs to be provided.

Africa, which resulted in significant delays and further pre-sale restructurings. Ultimately the purchaser was able to walk away from the sale.

It may be inappropriate in this situation to flag in the potential savings in the Information Memorandum, but providing the analysis to allow the bidder to do so is important. During the process whereby the bidder prepares their Non-binding Indicative Offer, the advisor can highlight the potential savings, either through meetings, or through separate correspondence, such as in the Process Letter (refer page 82). Bidders are usually hesitant to 'pay away' the benefits of some of the synergies they bring, but knowing they are in a competitive process, with other bidders, can result in portion of the synergistic benefits being paid away by the buyer as a premium to outbid others. This is therefore an important strategy to drive price higher in the bidding process.

Redacting information in an Information Memorandum

Depending on the bidder profile, it might be necessary to limit the disclosure of certain information. This may either be due to competition law concerns, or due to the commercial sensitivity of sharing certain strategic information. Certainly where competitors are approached, it would usually be appropriate to redact some information. For example, disclosure of revenue for larger customers may be particularly damaging if disclosed to a competitor, but may be important to give bidders an appreciation of customer concentration. In these cases redacting of customer names can assist.

Whilst an NDA will be in place to protect the target company, it may be advisable that a further precaution is taking by redacting customer information. This can take the form of deleting or black lining the names of customers in the Information Memorandum. For example, in list of top ten customers, listing the customers as Customer A, Customer B, Customer C etc. An alternative could be to include a high-level analysis of customers, such as "the top 5 customers constitute 45% of sales".

Management buy-out considerations in an Information Memorandum

Complexity is added to a sale process if financial buyers are participating. A critical risk when dealing with financial buyers is that management may be tainted – if they have an interest in participating alongside the private equity investor - and potentially incentivized to undersell the opportunity. They may even have had contact with one or more potential private equity firms in advance of the formal tender process. Often private equity firms are against the appointment of sell side advisors, and against competitive tender processes, and they often aggressively target management teams in advance to try and avert an auction process.

In addition to managing this inherent conflict, there are a number of practical information requirements that should be considered in preparing the Information Memorandum for presentation of an opportunity to financial buyers. Some of these include:

Cash flow

For private equity firms, cash flow is generally an important consideration. Often their investment case models are based in cash flow IRRs, and it is therefore important to provide robust forecasts which clearly indicate cash flows, together with well thought through capital expenditure forecasts.

Debt capacity

Low leverage, and the ability to access assets and cash flows to support acquisition finance at a low cost are important to a private equity buyer.

Managements' intention

Management are often important for buyers, but in the case of a trade buyer, the buyers own management team may be heavily involved in managing the business going forward. This is not the case in provide equity. A well-presented 'management' section of the Information Memorandum is always important but giving a sense of the management teams' continuity and commitment going forward is particularly relevant for private equity buyers. A younger, 'hungrier' management team is clearly an advantage in this case.

Stapled finance

A key process in any private equity transaction is considering the funding thereof. Most private equity investment is premised on the optimizing of the capital structure, through funding a significant proportion of the acquisition through debt. In order for a prospective private equity bidder to arrive at a meaningful Non-binding Indicative Offer, they would typically have to get a term sheet for debt finance from a bank. As a minimum, the Information Memorandum should therefore include all the information that would be required for a bank to determine their capacity and appetite to provide acquisition finance. Information required would include historical audited financials, full details of existing debt, future capex, historical and forecast free cash flow information, and details of all assets available for encumbrance.

It is counter-productive to have multiple financial bidders speaking to banks around the acquisition finance, especially at the indicative offer phase. It may therefore be useful for the advisor to share the Information Memorandum with some of the prospective banks who may provide acquisition finance, to get a view on the likely appetite, pricing and terms for acquisition finance. This can be done through a mini competitive process, procuring quotations (based on a draft Information Memorandum) from a number of financial institutions, and selecting one whose definitive terms are attached or 'stapled' to the Information Memorandum, on the basis that the terms have been determined by the bank prior to (and therefore, subject to) Due Diligence.

Where a Vendor Due Diligence is being performed, they may even have some useful suggestions in terms for the scope of the Due Diligence. If the Vendor Due Diligence is completed in advance of the finalization of the Information Memorandum and the stapled debt terms, the bank can get greater comfort in advance of circulating the stapled debt terms.

First prize is for the bank to agree to terms, if possible approved by their credit committee. It is important that these terms are credit approved or at least indicatively approved by credit as we have seen numerous instances where the terms of the deal have changed after a formal credit process. This could complicate the process considerably especially if the bidder is placing reliance on the stapled debt package to determine their bid price. These terms can then be used by a private equity firm to determine their offer price, which will be premised on the introduction of an element of acquisition finance.

Having a bank assess the credit appetite and approve the finance (even a preliminary approval) makes the bidding process much easier for a prospective financial buyer to arrive at an indicative offer and limits interactions between financial buyers and banks during the indicative offer phase, potentially making it possible to have a more accelerated Non-binding Indicative Offer Phase.

However the nature of the assessment by the bank is based purely on the debt capacity of the target, and the assessment is necessarily without reference to the prospective buyer. This can be a problem for some banks who would necessarily require the details of the financial sponsor before committing to finance.

One way to circumvent this concern is for the bank to review the bidder Short List, and conditionally approve the parties whom they would be comfortable to share their term sheet with. In this case the stapled debt package would not be included in the generic Information Memorandum, but 'stapled' to the Process Letter which is distributed to those parties the bank is comfortable with.

Exit

Question: Why did the private equity fund manager walk into the cinema backwards; Answer: Because he was looking for an exit!

Financial buyers, particularly those which run closed ended limited duration funds, are constrained by the need to exit their funds. Funds generally have a life span of between eight and ten years. Depending on when in the life an investment is made, private equity investors generally therefore look to exit their investments within a period of four to seven years. Accordingly, a critical consideration is the likelihood of being able to exit the business, through a listing or a follow-on sale, preferably to trade buyer (who would more likely pay a strategic premium) or to another financial buyers (a so-called secondary private equity deal).

Although dealing with the exit is not part of the Information Memorandum, when dealing with financial advisors, this is a key consideration that needs to be communicated in dealings with financial buyers.

Believing one's own story

Part of the job of any advisor worth their salt, is to present the opportunity in the most favorable light. However, it is important for sellers to retain some perspective in relation to their expectations. Sellers, particularly owner managers run the risk of factoring in the favorable messaging into their expectation of the business and the value. Therefore, whilst working to present a favorable outlook of the business, advisors are advised to temper expectations, and sellers advised to take heed this guidance.

6. The Vendor Due Diligence

Benefits of a Vendor Due Diligence

It was historically considered a conflict for a vendor to commission a Due Diligence for the benefit of prospective buyers, with bidders in a competitive process not placing reliance on the work performed by the sellers' advisors and hiring their own advisors to perform their Due Diligence investigations. However, the process of commissioning a Due Diligence is a considerable cost to any prospective buyer, a cost that has to be borne at the risk of not being selected as a preferred bidder. This is often a constraint for a buyer participating in a competitive sale process. This is particularly acute for some financial investors.

Not only is this process costly for the prospective buyer, it is also excessively burdensome for the seller in that they have to provide information, access and Q&A to each bidders Due Diligence team. These are often large teams of accountants, tax advisors and legal advisors, requiring access to significant information, and critically, detailed management interactions. A competitive process with, say, four bidders can therefore become extremely burdensome on the seller, and necessarily results in excessive duplication of activities by each bidders Due Diligence advisors.

This situation is further exacerbated today, by the limited number of large accounting firms available to hire for Due Diligence services. Following an era of mega-mergers in the accounting profession, and later, the collapse of Arthur Anderson (following the Enron scandal), the large accounting firms have consolidated into four behemoths. Whilst these firms' internal processes allow for Chinese walls to protect against conflicts of interests, where they advise more than one bidder in a process, there is nevertheless circumspection from investors, and a reticence to these solutions.

Vendor Due Diligence costs

As a result of the above and in the interests of expedience, accounting firms have developed the Vendor Due Diligence, a product designed to eliminate the shortcomings associated with the traditional buyer commissioned Due Diligence. The principle behind the Vendor Due Diligence is that it is commissioned for the benefit of all prospective bidders in a Due Diligence process.

Usually the Process Letter (refer page 81) issued to prospective bidders will advise bidders that a Vendor Due Diligence has been commissioned and paid for by the vendor. Often, the bidders will be required to undertake, as a condition to their gaining access to the Vendor Due Diligence, to pick up the cost of the Vendor Due Diligence in the event that they ultimately pick conclude a transaction. The cost of the Vendor Due Diligence is typically advised to prospective bidders up front, together with the scope.

Whilst the Vendor Due Diligence has clear benefits for the buyer and the seller, it does require the up-front investment to be made by the vendor. Accordingly, the seller effectively underwrites the cost as in the event of a failed process, the cost is for the account of the seller. In certain circumstances if there is some trepidation by the sellers, they can, at the time of initial approaches to bidders, ascertain through their sell side advisor, the appetite and interest from bidders for a Vendor Due Diligence. This provides the comfort to the seller that there will be acceptance of the independence of the report, and a willingness amongst bidders to ultimately pick up the cost of the Vendor Due Diligence (if ultimately successful). However it does mean that the timing of the initiation of the Vendor Due Diligence may be delayed beyond what is the optimal time (see below – Timing of Vendor Due Diligence)

In order to manage any perceived conflict, the accounting firm performing the Vendor Due Diligence typically 'signs over' the report to the ultimate purchaser, effectively providing the comfort required and the contractual rights afforded to any person who would commission the Vendor Due Diligence.

Bidders views of Vendor Due Diligence

There are differing views amongst bidders on the value of the Vendor Due Diligence. There was initially circumspection, particularly around the perceived conflict of interest, but over time there has been an increased acceptance of the Vendor Due Diligence product

One development in terms of services offered is the development of 'Data Book' services. This is where an accounting firm provides all the data and analysis required for the Due Diligence, without actually providing any assurance/comfort, or opinions. Accordingly, the information provided in a Data Book does not purport to provide comfort to the bidder, but nevertheless provides the required core information in a format which facilitates a quicker and more efficient Due Diligence process.

In general, there has been an increased acceptance of the Vendor Due Diligence. The product is particularly of interest to financial investors who don't have the capacity to commission multiple Due Diligence investigations on all deals where they participate in an auction process.

Timing of the Vendor Due Diligence

Typically, a Vendor Due Diligence should be commissioned by the seller during the Planning Phase, with a view to substantially finalizing the Vendor Due Diligence report before the issue of the Information Memorandum. The benefit of this timing is that it allows for management to provide input and commentary on the Vendor Due Diligence report and to take remedial actions for any adverse findings, before the initiation of the sale process. In addition, to the extent there are negative findings, the impact on the Information Memorandum can be considered. Although the Information Memorandums serves a different purpose, as the principle marketing document, and is therefore not purporting to be independent, it is counter-productive if there are clear contradiction between the Information memorandum and the Due Diligence report. Normally risks which are flagged in any Due Diligence report, should also be mentioned in the Information Memorandum, although in that document clear mitigating factors would typically also be highlighted.

Independence considerations in selecting a Vendor Due Diligence service provider

When selecting a service provider to provide the Vendor Due Diligence Services, acceptance of the report by the buyer universe should be a key consideration. Accordingly, the selected service provider should typically be a 'Big Four' accounting firm to ensure broad acceptance of the product by a diverse range of bidders. Where one is using a Big Four firm as ones sell side M&A advisor, the benefits of a familiarity and seamless service, which should not be underestimated, needs to be balanced against the conflict of interest – perceived by bidders - that may take place between the role of sell side advisor, which is remunerated by the seller on a successful sale, and the role of the Vendor Due Diligence service provider who is required to provide independent, objective, advice.

Top-up Due Diligence reporting

A key shortcoming of the Vendor Due Diligence is that the scope is set by the seller and would not take into account particular scoping requirements for acquirers. By its nature the scope of a Vendor Due Diligence is generic.

The Vendor Due Diligence is generally completed during the planning stage but is often supplemented by the buyers on advisors providing a Top-up Due Diligence, involving limited additional procedures that particular buyers would want to have addressed over and above the generic scope. This is dealt with in Chapter 8.

7. The Non-binding Indicative Offer Phase; Communication with Bidders and Managing the Contact Programme

The Process Letter

On receipt of a signed NDA, the sellers' advisors will distribute the Information Memorandum under cover of a Process Letter. Sometimes this Process Letter is referred to as Process letter 1, to differentiate it from Process Letter 2, which is issued to shortlisted bidders invited to participate in the Due Diligence phase. Unlike the generic Information Memorandum, which is typically the same document distributed to all bidders, the Process Letter is specifically addressed to the recipient bidder and may be customized. The role of the Process Letter is to:
- Explain the bidding timetable/ process, and
- Highlight the requirements for the Non-binding Indicative Offer.

In North America, a Non-Binding Indicative offer is sometimes referred to as an Indication of Interest.

Set out below are the key aspects which should be covered in the Process Letter.

Timing

In addition to highlighting the date by which the Non-binding Indicative Offer is due, it is advisable to give prospective bidders a sense of the timing of the subsequent Due Diligence phase, including the likely timing of management presentations, site visits and ancillary expert sessions. This will assist bidders in planning for their Due Diligence, including the appointment of external advisors which may be required for the Due Diligence. Sharing this timing is particularly important for international bidders to facilitate the planning of their travel in anticipation of being shortlisted.

The timing for the receipt of Non-binding Indicative Offers is typically set to allow for a period of three to four weeks, but in some cases, depending on the specific nature of bidders and their requirements to prepare Non-binding Indicative Offers, a longer period may be allowed. An extended period would usually be considered to allow for the specific governance approval processes anticipated for bidders. By its nature, the Non-binding Indicative Offer is based solely on the information in the Information Memorandum, and without access to management, so it is typically a short desk-top exercise. An exception may be considered if the nature of the business is such that the business site is particularly important for the evaluation of the opportunity (for example, a unique manufacturing facility), and access by many potential investors would not compromise the ongoing operations of the business.

Vendor Due Diligence

The Process Letter should indicate whether or not a vendor Due Diligence will be commissioned, and what the cost are if the intention is to recover this from the bidder. Whilst the Vendor Due Diligence will typically not be available during the Non-binding Indicative Offer Phase, information about the Vendor Due Diligence, including the proposed scope, can be shared with bidders to help them plan their potential Due Diligence, should they be shortlisted.

Terms of sale

The details of what is actually for sale should be stipulated, including the percentage stake for sale in the case of a share disposal. In the case of a sale of asset, the details of the specific assets should be provided, linking to an assumed take-on balance sheet.

Communications relating to the process

During the Non-binding Indicative Offer Phase of a sale process, the sellers' advisors will typically be dealing with a large number of potential buyers. Accordingly contact with management and access to the business should not be allowed. A well-prepared Information Memorandum should include all information required for a desk-top evaluation. On rare occasions the advisors may want to allow for limited requests for additional information, but these should be handled through the advisors.

Format of Non-binding Indicative Offer

Regarding the Non-binding Indicative Offer (in North America, the equivalent document is referred to as an Indication of Interest), the Process Letter should set out clearly the expectations of the seller with regards to the Non-binding Indicative Offer.

This would typically include:

Price

The Process Letter should request that the price is clearly set out. In order to ensure comparability between Indicative Offers, the basis of determination of price should be clearly stipulated. Normally one would request that bidders assume a uniform transaction date and balance sheet date. Typically, this would be the most recent balance sheet reporting date presented in the Information Memorandum. In order to ensure comparability of offers, the Process Letter should clearly stipulate the treatment of debt and cash. Typically, bidders would be requested to submit their offer based on an Enterprise Value, i.e. on a debt free and cash free basis.

Deal structure

Depending on the nature of the business being sold, sellers typically have a preference for the sale of shares, rather than a sale of assets. This is driven both by the complexity and timing with regards to concluding an asset deal, as well as potentially adverse tax consequences resulting from a the sale of assets, which could include the recoupment of capital allowances claimed on depreciated assets.

However in some cases, only a sale of assets would be possible (for example if an unincorporated division is being sold). Either way, guidance should be provided on the sellers' preference, and the Process Letter should request that the Non-binding Indicative Offer clearly stipulates the preferred deal structure.

In some instances, there may be an expectation that some bidders will not be able to propose an acquisition of shares. This may be the case with certain financial buyers, where a significant portion of the purchase consideration is to be financed through debt, or where a buyer is not prepared to take legacy liability associated with an incorporated entity.

In these cases, rather than preclude bidders from submitting an Non-binding Indicative Offer, one can stipulate that the sellers preference is for a sale of shares, but that bidders may submit an offer for assets, on the basis that when evaluating Non-binding Indicative Offers, any proposal for the acquisition of assets will be assessed against the adjusted net after tax proceeds relative to a sale of shares. There are also implications for the SPA when considering a sale of shares as opposed to a sale of assets. These are discussed in Chapter 10, specifically page 137.

Sale of component parts of a business

In certain circumstances, the sale may include a package which may be bid for individually and/ or in aggregate. This may occur where two divisions are being sold which could potentially be operated separately, or where the business operates from a property which may be sold separately from the operating business.

In this case adequate disaggregated financial information should be provided in the Information Memorandum to allow for separate bids, and bidders should be clearly directed on how to respond.

Basis of valuation

This should be requested, as it is sometimes useful for the seller to understand the basis used by the buyer to determine their purchase price, as it will inform the seller as to the sensitivities to be managed during due diligence.

Source of financing

Bidders should be requested to clearly stipulate how the proposed purchase price is to be financed. Where the bidder is to propose to pay the consideration out of its own resources, or where on balance sheet funding is to be secured, this should be supported by the balance sheet of the bidder to assist the seller in its evaluation of the bidders' creditworthiness. Where financing is required from a third party, this should be supported by a letter of support from a financial institution. The proportion of the purchase price to be funded from debt should be clearly stipulated.

Further approvals required

In order to estimate the timing to completion, the bidders' approval process should be requested.

Due Diligence required

It is useful to have an understanding of the Due Diligence required by the purchaser. The timing of the Due Diligence is normally stipulated by the seller, but by stipulating their Due Diligence procedures, the sellers' advisors can better prepare the data room and management presentations with the knowledge of the scope and extent of the planned Due Diligence process.

Confirmation of acceptance of terms of Vendor Due Diligence

Where a Vendor Due Diligence (VDD) has been commissioned, prospective bidders should be accordingly advised in the Process Letter that's a VDD report will be made available. As the VDD is commissioned for the benefit of prospective bidders, it is not uncommon that it is a requirement for bidders to confirm their agreement to pick up the cost of the VDD, in the event that they are ultimately the successful bidder.

Strategic rationale

Understanding the rationale for an acquisition can be useful to assess the levers for value for the prospective buyer. In addition, the seller may have an interest in a continuing relationship with the buyer, and in the continued success of the business, especially if the seller is a multi-national holding company who may continue to supply the business.

CASE STUDY: When value is not the primary driver for a transaction

Whilst value is normally the primary concern for a seller when contemplating a disposal, it is by no means the only driver, and in some cases, sales price is less important than other softer issues. The author is able to cite a number of examples.

When the author was a global European based bank was selling a non-core South African subsidiary, a key concern was its continuing relationship with the regulators and with political leadership in the country. The size and scale of the local business was so small, that sale proceeds were less important than being seen to be selling to a responsible seller who would continue to operate the business and mitigate any potential job losses.

Often when an owner manager sells a business the legacy left behind is key motivator. Ensuring the continuance of the company as a going concern and the retention of staff sometimes tips price when the owner manager considers a disposal.

The author has advised a Telco operator on the sale of its logistics division. The transaction, which was an asset transaction was evaluated not on the price at which the assets were sold, but on the terms of the continued outsource agreement in place.

These are a few examples where price is a subsidiary concern to other matters. Where important, these matters should be clearly articulated in the Process Letter.

Anticipated regulatory approvals required from the buyers side

Prior to the selection of prospective bidders, it is useful to assess the possibility of regulatory hurdles, including anti-trust issues. In some cases, however, it may not be possible to fully anticipate whether there would be competition law concerns in advance of approaching prospective bidders. In such cases the Process Letter should be tailored for the particular recipient where there is a potential concern, such that there is a clear request that the relevant information (For example, market share data for the buyer) is provided, together with the bidders view on the likelihood of regulatory approval for the transaction.

Intentions for management

Clearly management will be meeting the bidder during the Due Diligence process. Therefore understanding the intentions that the buyer has for management is important in order to manage the subsequent Due Diligence process, and in particular management interactions during management presentations and site visits.

Details of the bidders advisors

Understanding the advisors is important to ensure that the bidder is able to manage conflicts of interest which may arise through having the same firm potentially advising more than one bidder. This is particularly a risk in the area of financial Due Diligence advisors, where only four large accounting firms exist to service the market.

Disclaimer

It is critically important to include a disclaimer, clearly advising the recipient that the seller retains complete unfettered discretion and the right to change or terminate the process, and not accept the highest price. Typically, this type of disclaimer would be sufficient for a private company, but for certain public listed entities, there may be additional laws and regulations governing any sale process which would impose an obligation to treat all parties fairly, and reduce the discretion a non-listed sellers would have. In these cases, a fair and transparent process may be critical, and the advisors should take particular care in this regard.

Although the Information Memorandum has joint flavor and input, with management playing a critical role in its preparation, the Information Memorandum is usually branded with the advisor's letterhead/ logo. Although it is management's story, it is important that the advisors are seen to be controlling the process. Contact between management and bidders should not be allowed during the initial phases of the process as the Non-binding Indicative Offer is prepared, and the branding of the document with the advisor logo/ letterhead emphasizes the important message that contact should only be with the advisor.

Profit warranties

The presentation of favorable forecasts of a business is often done with a view to drive up the valuation. Where bidders are struggling to agree to the forecasts, a possible way to bridge the gap is through a deferred purchase price linked to the future financial performance (often referred to as a profit warranty). Particularly where a seller is confident of the business achieving its forecast profit, a profit warranty can be a useful tool to bridge the gap between the seller's price expectations and those of a buyer. Where a seller is confident about the future performance and is prepared to warrant this, consideration should be given to advise bidders up front, prior to submitting their offer, as it will likely result in higher price. Whilst this is probably not something for the information memorandum, it should be communicated, either in the process letter, or verbally by the advisor to the bidder.

Managing the contact program

Issuing of NDA and Teaser

Having agreed to a list of bidders, ones advisors are typically tasked with making contact with them to share the details of the target opportunity. One exception to this would be where the seller has had previous approaches from, or has an existing relationship with, prospective bidders. In these situations, it may be appropriate that initial contact be made by the seller, but once contact has been made future interaction should always be with the advisors to the seller. This ensure the integrity of the process is maintained.

Contact may take the form of an email approach, sharing the teaser and the Non-Disclosure Agreement (NDA). However, a direct telephone approach by the advisor is also good to establish rapport with the prospective seller and gauge preliminary interest in the opportunity.

As a first step, a short Teaser (as described on page 55) is sent, together with a NDA.

Typically, a non-disclosure agreement requires some discussion and negotiation with the prospective buyers' legal advisors or in-house council. The process of making contact with bidders and negotiating the NDA can take a week or two and so this time should be catered for in the timetable.

Chapter 5 sets out the typical terms of a NDA, as well as the process to be followed when negotiating changes thereto.

Communication with employees and other interested parties

Notwithstanding the negotiation of non-disclosure agreements, once the contact program is initiated, information about the sale process could begin to leak to employees, customers and suppliers of the business.

It is therefore advisable, on initiation of the contact program, to agree on some communication with employees and other key parties, if the leak in relation to the potential sale process could be damaging to the business. This is always a better form of communications than unsubstantiated rumors which may arise from other sources. The communications should, to the extent appropriate, reassure employees around the safety of their continued employment.

Use of a contact programme register

During the contact program, often a number of personnel are used to make contact with buyers, particularly if there are a large number of bidders to contact. In globally coordinated sale processes, the number of buyers could exceed 50. Particularly where international buyers are being contacted, the advisor may use key personnel in another office to make contact with prospective buyers. It is important that the contact is made within the right level of the bidders' organization to ensure a prompt and meaningful response.

It is also important that discussions details are fed back, and the contact program is properly documented. Negative responses received from prospective buyers can be informative to better understanding a general trend of the markets response to the opportunity.

Accordingly, a proper contact program register should be maintained by the advisors. Typically a contact program register would include:
- Date contact made;
- Nature of contacts (call/ email);
- Date of response;
- Date NDA received back;
- Any significant amendments to template NDA;
- Date of withdrawal from process, together with rationale for withdrawal;
- Date of receipt of Non-binding Indicative Offer;
- Key discussion points from last contact with bidder;
- In the event of termination, confirmation of return and/ or destruction of confidential information.

In addition to recording interactions around the NDA and the Teaser, the date of distribution of the Information Memorandum should be recorded, together with any subsequent interactions during the indicative offer phase. Clearly all NDA received should be properly filed for posterity.

Tracking the IM

The IM is usually watermarked of uniquely numbered so that the version is attributable to a particular bidder. This is a control to ensure that the Information Memorandum only goes to those parties for whom it is intended, and to ensure that the sellers' advisors retain control over the process.

Contact between bidders and management during the Non-binding Indicative Offer Phase

By its very nature, the competitive auction process is designed to restrict bidder contact with management during the Indicative Offer Phase. Furthermore, a properly prepared Information Memorandum will provide all the information typically required to determine a valuation and prepare a Non-binding Indicative Offer. Notwithstanding this, the advisor should maintain contact with the bidders. Typically, around three clear weeks is allowed for the bidder to evaluate the Information Memorandum and respond with a Non-binding Indicative Offer. During week two, the advisor should contact bidders to confirm their interest, and remind them of the deadline date for receipt of Non-binding Indicative Offers. Where further information is requested this should be considered, based on who the bidder is, and if a response is required, or more information provided, this should be facilitated though the seller's advisors.

Receipt and evaluation of Non-binding Indicative Offers

Assuming there are no governance approval processes and a seller's deal team is able to make a decision without recourse to external board or investment committee approvals, a week should be provided to evaluate and conclude on indicative offers. However a longer period may be required if recommendations need to be separately approved by an investment committee.

In the absence of third party approvals, a period of a week allows for the extension of receipt by a few days, and also affords the seller and their advisors to request further information from bidders and/ or seek clarification on their offers before deciding on a shortlist.

Offers should be evaluated alongside each other considering the response to key issues (refer to Process Letter above). In addition to price, careful consideration should be given to each bidder's ability to fund and close the deal. The process of reviewing offers and considering a shortlist for selection for Due Diligence is discussed further in Chapter 8.

8. The Due Diligence Phase

Selection of preferred bidders

Selecting shortlist for Due Diligence

The objective behind the structured and phased bidding process is to eliminate, at an early stage, parties who are not considered serious contenders for the acquisition of the target business. Assuming a well-prepared Information Memorandum is provided to bidders, the preparation of a Non-binding Indicative Offer is not particularly onerous on the target and its management team, as is it a desktop exercise performed by bidders, without any interaction with the management of the target. Typically, the advisors would deal with any enquiries and discussions at the Non-binding Indicative Offer Phase. Whilst there may be requests for further information and even discussions with management, these are generally limited.

However, the Due Diligence phase of the process is much more taxing on the target and its management team. The Due Diligence phase, which typically lasts for between five and seven weeks (depending on the complexity of the business) requires significant input from management for management presentations, sessions with target company experts such as legal, HR and Finance (so called 'expert sessions'), and general responses to Q&A. In addition, although the sellers and their advisors would have compiled a comprehensive data room, there are typically numerous additional information requests, from bidders and their Due Diligence advisors.

Accordingly, it is important to ensure a manageable amount of parties are invited to participate in the Due Diligence phase, whilst at the same time retaining the competitive tension associated with multiple bidders in a process. One can also reasonably expect some shortlisted parties to fall out during Due Diligence, so one should ideally have a minimum of three parties in the process. Managing more than four or five parties in Due Diligence becomes complex for the seller, so the ideal number of parties is generally three or four.

If you have very good bidders, and the seller is confident is can close with one of three preferred bidders who have offered an acceptable price, then three, or even two bidders may suffice.

When a Vendor Due Diligence is available, one should hope, if it is comprehensive and well prepared, that the Due Diligence process by the bidders will be less intrusive and complex as they will place an element of reliance on the Vendor Due Diligence. In such situations, a larger number of bidders may be accommodated, as their Due Diligence procedures will hopefully be limited to 'top up' Due Diligence.

Top-Up Due Diligence

Notwithstanding the obvious value of the Vendor Due Diligence, which has seen its growth in popularity, it should be recognized that each bidder in a Due Diligence process will have their own unique issues that they want to focus on. Accordingly, the scope of the Vendor Due Diligence should be reasonably comprehensive, but a buyer will often require that a Top-Up Due Diligence. Typically, the Top-Up Due Diligence service provider will be a party independent of the Vendor Due Diligence service provider. The latter being commissioned by the vendor. This is to provide an element of objectivity and independence to the work performed by the VDD service provider.

The stalking horse

In desperate situations where there is only one credible bidder, one should consider the inclusion of a second or third bidder, even if their offer is not considered credible, the inclusion of such a party as a 'stalking horse' can assist in maintaining the competitive tension which may not otherwise be there.

Treating bidders fairly

Generally, in a managed disposal process, the seller is not in any way constrained or obliged to treat parties fairly. Typically, the Process Letters and Information Memorandum make it clear that he decisions are at the sole and complete discretion of the seller, without any recourse from any unsuccessful bidder. However, there are circumstances, particularly in regulated industries and in disposals by public sector entities, where laws may require that there is equity in the treatment of bidders and this should be kept in mind. In particular the selection should be measured against predetermined and communicated criterion per the Process Letter 1 (which is dealt with in chapter 7).

In addition, there are ethical considerations, it is generally considered unfair to share the prices received from one bidder to another. Sometimes, when marking up a Non-disclosure Agreement (NDA), a bidder will request that the seller undertakes to keep any and all information received from the bidder as confidential so in dealing with other parties, the seller should be mindful of adhering to these obligations.

Rationale for selection

Your Process Letter 1, which is issued on signature of the NDA (and dealt with in Chapter 7) will typically set out the basis under which parties should respond, and against which they should be evaluated.

Typically, the various criterion relates to one of three key objectives which form the basis of selection:

- Value;
- Certainty, and
- Timing.

Value

Clearly the purchase price is a key aspect in the evaluation of any bid. Care should be taken in evaluating an offer to ensure that the bidder has clearly demonstrated an understanding of the reconciliation of Enterprise Value to Equity Value, as this can result in a misunderstanding of the value of the Non-binding Indicative Offer.

Particularly with the Non-binding Indicative Offer Phase, one should be circumspect in the assessment of overly flattering valuations. They are often used to get into the DD phase, but upon further enquiry the other two factors below are lacking. They also sometimes demonstrate a lack of understanding of the business.

Certainty

A careful evaluation of the offer and the offeror should be done to determine their capacity to execute given their financial resources and approvals required. Care should be taken not to exclude credible bidders at a lower price, for higher valued whimsical offers, which are unlikely to be able to be concluded, because for example, the offer is subject to finance and/ or shareholder approval by the bidders.

A further consideration in evaluation of offers is the likelihood of regulatory interventions. This may include the sector regulators (particularly in highly regulated sectors such as banking and insurance), but also completion law regulators, who would consider the impact a potential transaction may have on the competitive environment.

Timing

Linked to uncertainty is timing, and typically a longer due diligence and/ or approval process required by the seller should be poorly viewed. A longer approval timetable creates uncertainty and increases the likelihood of deal failure.

War Story: Sale of pan-African business

The author was hired to assist in the sale of business with its legal head office in Mauritius and its operational head office in South Africa, but with its operations in many African countries.
The key bidder that emerged was another group, with similar operations in West Africa. One of the approvals required was that of the West Africa Economic and Monetary Union (CEMAC) Competition Commission.

The timing and process to follow was unclear, but the clear legal advice was that the process could not be approved without the approval of the CEMAC Competition Commission which could take up to seven months. In the interim the business suffered due to the recessionary environment in many of the countries where it operated.

Notwithstanding a binding contract, due to the elapse of time, and failure to complete contractual conditions precedent, within the required time frame, the bidder was able to renegotiate the terms and ultimately walk away from the transaction.

The moral of the story is that a significant delay imposed by regulatory processes and approvals can sink a deal, and any required regulatory approvals should be carefully considered in assessing any offer.

Messaging to shortlisted parties

Where parties are invited to participate, it is sometimes good to provide verbal feedback when advising them of their shortlisting. Especially where there is strong interest and attractive pricing, it may be good to advise bidders that whilst the offer is good in other aspects, their proposed price in their Final Offer would need to be more attractive to secure the deal.

Process Letter 2

Once a shortlist of preferred bidders is selected to participate in the Due Diligence process, a further process letter is prepared. The purpose of this letter, which is generally issued by the sellers' advisors, is to inform the bidder of their selection as a preferred bidder, and also to guide them with regards to the timing of Due Diligence and process up to the submission of Final Offers.

The Process Letter 2 typically addresses the following matters:

- Timing for Due Diligence;
- Details of proposed site visits;
- Details of access to virtual data room, including where applicable, access to Vendor Due Diligence reports;
- Where a vendor Due Diligence has been commissioned, a meeting with the Vendor Due Diligence preparer will typically be offered;
- Indicative timing for management presentations;
- Other sessions with management on key aspects of the business (often referred to as 'expert sessions') which would drill down into particular aspects of the business. This may include tax, finance, HR, and legal;
- Reference to the draft Sale and Purchase Agreement (SPA), which is typically provided to bidders to mark-up, and submitted in a form that is acceptable for the bidder;
- Q&A process to be followed, and
- Reference to the required form of the Final Offer: typically, this would be similar to that of indicative offer, but it would also include details of the proposed completion mechanism; Locked Box or Completion accounts.

The matters above, are further elaborated below.

In some cases, a separate Locked Box Letter is provided which sets our details of the requirements for the submission of the final offer together with details of working capital cyclicality and a reconciliation of Enterprise Value to Equity Value, for the purpose of assisting bidders in submitting their offer on the basis of Locked-Box Accounts.

Timing for Due Diligence

The timing of the Due Diligence phase is typically five to seven weeks. The timetable should allow for sufficient time for bidders to complete their Due Diligence and submit a final binding offer (Final Offer) which would typically include a mark-up of the final SPA (please refer to chapter 10). If a Vendor Due Diligence has been commissioned and is available, then a shorter period may be considered appropriate.

Another consideration in setting the timetable for Due Diligence is the nature of the bidders involved in a process. For international bidders, timetables should consider timing involved in travel, document translation (if required), and cater for the bidders anticipated approval timelines. Bidders that require financing may also require longer approval processes and this should be catered for in the timetable.

Site Visits

Site visits should be considered during the Due Diligence phase. For any manufacturing concern, this would typically include a walkthrough of the targets manufacturing facilities. As with management presentations, site visits should typically controlled, with access to one bidder at a time.

Access to Virtual Data Room, and Q&A process

Details of data room access will be provided to bidders (see below). In the process letter, bidders will also be requested to select a coordinator for the Q&A process which is typically facilitated through the Virtual Data Room portal, to allow for a record of all questions made and answers provided.

Completion accounts vs Locked box mechanism

The purchase of a business is typically subject to the completion of various Conditions Precedent. With increasing complexity of transactions and regulatory oversight (particularly anti-trust laws), the process to complete transactions is becoming more time consuming. There is often a considerable delay between the completion of Due Diligence, the signature of a definitive sale and purchase agreement, and the completion of the transaction when the conditions precedent are fulfilled.

Because of this, there needs to be a mechanism to adjust the price agreed on signature for subsequent events and/ or compensate the parties for the elapse of time which can be up to several months.

Completion accounts mechanism

One way to achieve this is the preparation of completion accounts. Using this methodology, the purchase price, which is paid on completion, is adjusted with reference to completion accounts which are completed at that time. Typically, a preliminary purchase price is determined based on the net assets to be acquired and referenced to a historical balance sheet. This would typically be the balance sheet at the last practicable date available at the time of the due diligence and may be referenced to the balance sheet covered in any Vendor Due Diligence report. This is subsequently adjusted when the transaction completes, based on any changes to the net asset on completion. In effect the risk/ rewards of the business lie with the seller until completion, as any movement in the value of the assets acquired are adjusted (upwards or downwards) in the final purchase consideration.

In some cases where the value of the fixed assets are not expected to change the purchase price adjustment is referenced to the value of the working capital (cash, stock, debtors and creditors).

The SPA needs to clearly define the basis for the determination of the preliminary purchase price, and clearly set out the mechanism for determining the adjustment to arrive at the final purchase price. A good idea is to append a schedule to the SPA which sets out the basis of determination to ensure a clear understanding of the computation of the preliminary purchase price. This helps clarify the basis and methodology which will be used to determine the final purchase price and therefore any adjustments to the purchase price to be paid after completion of the transaction.

Set out below is a diagrammatic presentation of the processes involved to achieve completion where the completion accounts mechanism is followed:

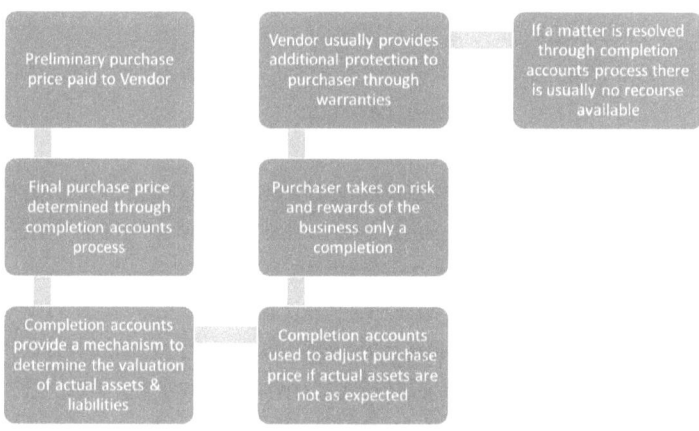

Locked box mechanism

The completion accounts mechanism necessitates the preparation of completion accounts to determine the final purchase price. This adds time and cost to the process and introduces an element of uncertainty with regards to the final purchase price. In order to eliminate this complexity, the locked box mechanism fixes the price of the business at the date of signature. The purchase price is normally determined with reference to a recent historical balance sheet, sometimes referred to as the Locked Box Accounts, with the reference date being referred to as the Locked Box Date.

In effect the buyer takes all the risks and rewards of ownership from the Locked Box Date, notwithstanding that completion will only take place sometime in the future. In the case of the sale of a profitable, cash generative business, as the buyer effectively assumes all profits from the Locked Box Date. The purchase price negotiated should therefore be higher and/ or an interest charge calculated from the Locked Box Date to the completion date.

This interest rate would be sufficient to compensate the seller for the lost profits. A seller would typically negotiate for a higher rate of interest calculated with reference to the return on equity, or use the buyers purchase price (EBITDA/ EV multiple) as a reference point to determine a rate of interest. For example, an EV/ EBITDA multiple of 8x would imply an interest rate of 12.5% which would typically be higher than prevailing interest rates, adequately compensating the seller for the anticipated profits the buyer would earn from the business between signature and completion. Calculating an interest charge on this obviously requires the buyer and seller to have a reasonably firm view on the expected/ budgeted earnings which are anticipated post the signature of the SPA.

When agreeing to a locked box mechanism, as the buyer assumes risk and rewards of the business from the Locked Box Date, so there is a need for increased warranties to be provided by the seller with respect to the treatment of the business in the interim period, to protect the purchaser from value stripping. This would include a moratorium on dividends during the interim period.

The use of a locked box mechanism does require an element of trust between the buyer and seller.

Set out below is a diagrammatic presentation of the processes involved to achieve completion where the locked box mechanism is followed:

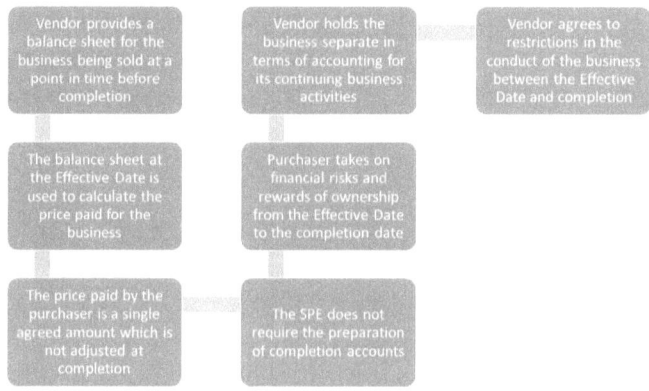

Below is an overview of the typical timelines involved in a hypothetical transaction comparing the timing under the two different processes, locked box versus completion accounts.

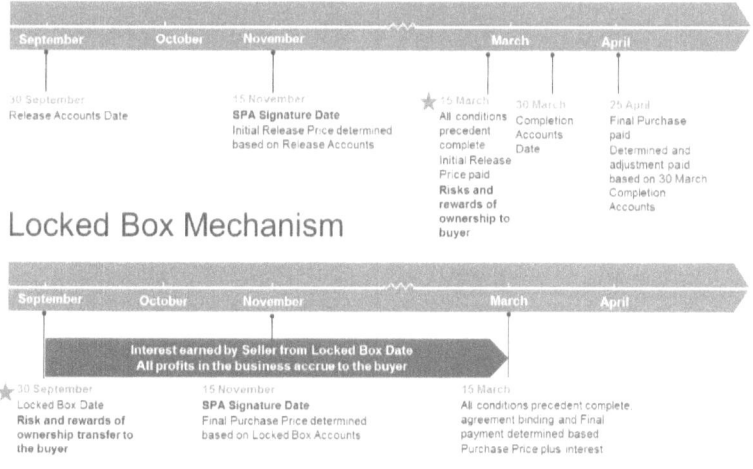

Data Room Preparation

During the compilation of the Information Memorandum and the Teaser, the sellers' advisors would typically begin to compile the data room. The data room is usually handled through a secure portal managed by a third party.

What information to provide in a data room

The process of selecting a long list of prospective bidders, narrowing this to a short list, and then only selecting parties for due diligence who have provided competitive Non-binding Indicative Offers is designed to accommodate only parties with serious intent, acceptable valuation and capacity to execute on an acquisition.

With the objective of receiving Final Offers, it is therefore recommended that, subject to particular concerns over confidentiality and any legal restrictions on sharing information, a comprehensive data room is provided, with any and all information that a bidders may require to make a final investment decision, and submit a Final Offer. Where third party contracts have confidentiality clauses, those parties should be contacted to procure their consent for the release of the contracts into the data room.

Use of Third Party administered Virtual Data Rooms

A number of service providers provide outsourced secure portals to manage the documentation flows in confidential transactions. The features of these virtual data rooms provide for different levels of access security depending on the client's preference and concerns over client confidentiality and allow for facilitated confidential Q&A through the portal.

User access can range from only allowing view only access, to allowing full download and print functionality for all documents on the data room. Other features allow for the inclusion of watermarks, which clearly indicate the bidders' details on any documents downloaded to ensure traceability of any misdirected documents.

The functionality of these systems also provides for monitoring and reporting on activity by bidders and their advisors which is a useful tool to gauge activity and interest from prospective bidders.

It is often advised that numerical information (Such as management accounts, forecasts) are made available in excel format to allow for bidders and their advisors to readily and easily analyze the information provided, but there may be sensitivity in allowing the download of other commercially sensitive information (for example, customer contracts).

Treatment of commercially sensitive and confidential information

Depending on the nature of the bidders and the information being provided, it is often important that certain information is redacted or anonymized. This involves the deletion of sensitive aspects of information provided. This could include the removal of top customer names and the provision of anonymous descriptors (customer 1, customer 2, customer 3, And so on) to a list of top customers. In addition to commercial sensitivity, there may be reasons to redact certain employee data (For example salary) to comply with privacy laws.

In addition to the above, depending on the nature of the bidders, there may be a restriction on the type of commercial information a seller will be allowed to share with a competitor. This will be governed by anti-trust/ competition law in the jurisdiction of the target, the seller and the buyer.

When dealing with competitors it may be necessary to screen the due diligence team to ensure only appropriate members of the bidders management (not involved in strategic management) have access to the data room, and there may also be a need for a separate NDA (a 'clean room' NDA) to be signed with these management members. At this stage it would be important to seek legal advice on what it is appropriate to share with whom.

Confirmatory due diligence

Where there is a redaction of information, there may be a need to allow for a short confirmatory due diligence with the single preferred bidder after the acceptance of their Final Offer. For the purpose a separate data room is retained to share, on a fully transparent basis, all un-redacted information and any other particularly sensitive commercial information not disclosed through the preliminary due diligence process. This is sometimes referred to as a 'red data room'.

Signing off on the data room

Whilst the advisor can provide significant assistance with the collating of information, indexing and ordering, and the reviewing for reasonableness, the ultimate responsibility should remain with the seller and the company to confirm the veracity of the information on the data room and to agree to the opening the data room to bidders.

Posting the SPA on the data room

During the due diligence phase, the proposed SPA is typically posted by the seller into the data room. When submitting the final offer, bidders are typically requested to mark-up the SPA with their suggested amendments. Bidders should be advised that this will form part of the evaluation of their Final Offer, such that amendments to warranties, indemnities and other clauses form part of the evaluation of each bidders Final Offer. An understanding of the competitive tension is important, and bidders should be reminded that in addition to their Final Offer, excessive mark-ups to the draft SPA which transfer risk to the seller will be a factor in evaluating their Final Offer.

Sellers should also, however, appreciate that a one-sided contract may have implications on price, and my also result in a bidder walking away, so whilst the draft SPA shared with bidders should be acceptable to the seller, it should not be unduly prejudicial to the bidder. This situation will only cause tensions and unnecessary negotiation with a bidder during the final negotiations.

Management Presentations

Having been through a desk top exercise, to arrive at a Non-binding Indicative Offer, bidders will be keen to get into the heart of their investigations – quizzing the management team on their business. This often represents the most important part of the sales process, and many a transaction is made or broken during these management interactions. Accordingly, it is critical that the seller and the management team of the target prepares properly for these engagements.

Nature and timing of interactions

The Due Diligence process generally runs between four and six weeks, depending on the complexity of the business and the nature/ profile of the bidders. A consideration in the timetable for the Due Diligence is whether or not a Vendor Due Diligence is going to be made available by the sellers. Where a Vendor Due Diligence is provided, the timelines can be reduced, perhaps by two weeks. Sometimes trade buyers, particularly smaller/ owner managed businesses, are better placed to execute a speedy Due Diligence, sometimes with limited external advice. Typically, larger multinationals firms will run a more professional Due Diligence process, hiring an independent accounting firm (usually a Big Four), lawyers, and other external experts, for example environmental specialists in the case of a manufacturing business. Although private equity firms tout their ability to execute a speedy transaction, and they argue that their approval processes are quicker, their business model usually requires external debt funding, which adds complexity to the approvals required to arrive at a binding offer.

What is the appropriate timing for management presentations? In the author's view, it is preferable to have these interactions in the second or third week of the Due Diligence process. Ideally, bidders and their advisors, will want to peruse the data room, see what is available, and prepare adequately for the limited opportunity they will have to ask face to face questions of management. Many bidders will need to plan travel arrangements, and finalize the appointment of their advisors, making earlier management presentations difficult. One would be advised against management presentations towards the end of the Due Diligence process, as these sessions typically lead to further investigations and enquiries by bidders, accordingly one should at least allow for two weeks following management presentations for bidders to finalize their binding offers.

In addition to the high-level management presentation, it is usually advisable to have a number of ancillary meetings with parts of the management team. These are often referred to as 'expert sessions'. In a large and complex businesses, it is often not possible for subject matter experts such as finance professionals or Human Resources experts to drill down into an appropriate level of detail into the issues they wish to discuss. Therefore, in addition to a two to three hour management presentation, follow on sessions can be set up to discuss finance, human resources, legal, environmental issues, etc. This provides for the opportunity for the bidders Due Diligence team to interrogate functional executives on key issues of importance to their respective work streams. This also ensures that the management presentation does not get bogged down in what the strategic thinkers would view as operational matters, which are nevertheless important for the bidder in formulating a binding offer.

In addition to extra sessions with finance and human resources teams, the seller may want to afford bidders the opportunity to discuss the draft sale and purchase agreement. The nature of these discussions is usually aimed and clarifying the rationale for the basis of preparation, and explaining the thinking behind the structure of the SPA, including the methodology of the completion process, for example the locked box mechanism. Entering into specific negotiations should be avoided during this session, as the will typically be undertaken once a single preferred bidder is selected.

Preparation for management presentations

Over the years, the author has been continuously reminded that business managers are often ill prepared for the task of selling their business and for selling themselves as a management team. It is appropriate at this time for ones advisors to provide some guidance on what is required in a management presentation, but it is most important that the presentation has been primarily prepared by the management team to ensure the buy in and support of the parties who will be presenting. There can be nothing worse than a chief executive presenting something he has not had significant input into. My advice therefore is that the advisor prepares the skeleton of the presentation, and possibly advises on the format of the slides, but that the preparation should rest with the presenters, being the management team who will be speaking on the day.

Who should attend the management presentation?

From the seller, one should include representatives from the lead advisor, as well as a senior representative of the seller. Whilst the advisor's contribution to the presentation itself is limited, it represents a useful opportunity for the advisor to gauge, through questions asked by the bidder, the level of interest, as well as the potential negotiation issues down the line. From the nature of the interactions during the management presentations, the respective strengths of the bidding parties can be evaluated. In addition, any follow up issues requiring further sharing of information can be easily facilitated through the advisors if they are present in these interactions.

From the buyer, one would typically expect the lead of their M&A/ business development team, as well as some senior operational executives – hopefully the decision makers in their investment process. I have been involved in processes where the team leading the Due Diligence have invested significant time, and costs, only to find that their superiors scupper the transaction on the basis that the target did not meet the buying groups strategic objectives.

It is also useful that the representatives of the clients' advisors – Due Diligence advisors and M&A advisors are also present. In the case of financial buyers, it is also good to have representatives from the banks who may be providing the acquisition finance component of the purchase consideration. One should remember that the management presentation takes a considerable amount of investment in the targets senior leadership. Therefore, bidders should be encouraged to have a substantial team represented, to avoid unnecessary duplication of enquiries further on in the Due Diligence process. As there are often four of more parties shortlisted for Due Diligence process, it is valuable to the seller that the buyer is well represented, to limit further enquiries and follow up meetings.

Content of management presentation

In many respects the presentation will run through much of what has been provided in the Information Memorandum. It is critical that nothing is said which is contrary to the Information Memorandum, as this will create doubt in the bidder's mind about the veracity of all information provided by the seller. Unless there are compelling reasons, the forecasts presented should be the same as those in the Information Memorandum. Whilst some of those attending the management presentation would have read the Information Memorandum, it is likely that many of those attending will not have. It is therefore advisable not to assume a high level of knowledge from the audience, and much of what is presented will be a repeat of the Information Memorandum.

Typically, the management presentation would include the following:
- An introduction from the seller, explaining the rationale for the process;
- A history of the business, highlighting key milestones;
- An overview of the products and services – by division, if appropriate, with high level financial information;
- A historical financial overview of the business;
- Forecast, including key assumptions;
- What's not in the business plan – blue sky opportunities;
- Q&A time;
- At the end the advisors can provide an overview of the remaining timetable to completion, including details of further expert sessions.

It is best of the management presentation is delivered by the management who will be transferring with the business. The financial aspects should be delivered by the most senior financial executive, the chief executive should deliver the history and the overview of the products and services. Depending on the size of the business, divisional heads should also speak through their sections. It is generally advisable that all of management in the meeting participate in the presentation.

Care should be taken by the seller to introduce the opportunity with a cogent explanation of the strategic rationale for the disposal. Whilst the purpose of the management presentation is to paint a picture of how good the business is, it will often leave the bidder questioning why, if it is such a great business, is it being sold? A good answer is always one which relates to corporate decisions which have resulted in a change of strategic direction rather than the business of the target. Similarly, in the case of a privately owned business, succession can often be seen as a legitimate rationale for selling. Management should buy-in to this disposal rationale, it is counterproductive if, during Q&A, they contradict the seller.

As any buyer will attest, a management team can be the most important attribute in purchasing a business. This is particularly the case for private equity buyers. It is therefore advisable for a dry run. During this time the advisors will typically act as the bidders and prepare questions to grill the management on. In the author's experience, a proper dry run allows for a better presentation. The author has often seen, where there are three or four management presentations that the presentations improve dramatically through the process.

Presentation of forecast and future prospects is always a sensitive area. Sellers and their advisors should be cognizant of the often difficult and conflicted position management will find themselves in. They will recognize that they are presenting to their future bosses, and will be reluctant to oversell the prospects and the forecasts, knowing that they are likely to be held to account for these forecasts in the future.

During the management presentations, the management team will start to form a view of their preferred bidder. One should never forget that their interests are in forging a long-term career/ future. They will not be incentivized to sell at the highest price, in fact if a bidder overpays for the business, they will unlikely pay the price down the line. On some cases management may actively undermine the process by supporting a less favored bidder. This is particularly the case where one of the bidders may be a private equity firm, who would be seeking to partner with management as investors in the business.

For this reason, the seller, or at least their advisors, should be present at all meetings to manage this situation. Business cards should not be shared by management and at the commencement of the presentation, the bidders should be reminded by the seller's advisors, of their obligations set out in the signed Non-disclosure Agreement, and their commitment not to make any direct approach to the management. The management team should be equally instructed by the seller, that all approached/ enquiries should be directed to the sellers lead advisor.

It is common for a seller to offer each bidder the opportunity to enjoy a dinner with the management, the seller's advisors and the seller after the management presentation. This does run the risk of management increasing their familiarity with the bidders, but equally allows the seller to form a relationship with the bidder team and gauge the level of interest. It also allows for the seller to better understand the strategic rationale for the transaction. On balance, the dinner is usually a good idea. It is a useful mechanism for the seller and their advisors to learn more about the bidder, and get to grips with some of the softer issues which may have a bearing on negotiations down the line.

Alternatives to a two- phased sale process

The process outlined in this book is a typical two-phased process whereby an initial Non-binding Indicative Offer is solicited, following which a Due Diligence process is run with shortlisted bidders, leading to Final Offers, and the selection of a single preferred bidder with whom to enter into detailed negotiation of transaction agreements.

This process may often need to be tailored for the specific circumstances of a business and the nature of bidders is often a key consideration. Sometimes where it is expected that bidders will not be able to commit to due diligence (often the case with financial bidders), there may be merit in splitting the due diligence phase into two discrete components:
- One where shortlisted bidders are offered the opportunity to firm up on their Non-binding Indicative Offer, by providing further access to a Vendor Due Diligence, and possibly management presentations, and
- A further shortlist of bidders being provided full unfettered access to the data room for the purposes of a short confirmatory due diligence, following which Final Offers, with SPA mark-ups will be requested.

In some cases, adding this further phase to the process can facilitate more involvement from competing bidders, prior to the need for them to commit costs for the appointment external professional advisors.

9. Closing the Deal

Evaluation of final bids and selection of party for final negotiations

One is now at the stage of the sale process where a party is selected for final negotiations and conclusions. In Chapter 8, we discussed the evaluation of indicative offers and now it is time to once again evaluate offers against one and other and also against the Non-binding Indicative Offer which may have changed as a result of bidders' Due Diligence findings.

At this stage each bidders Due Diligence should be complete and as close as possible to a final and binding offer. Each bidder would also have been expected to have marked up the SPA and returned it in a form they are able to sign, subject to minimal negotiations.

In North America, the post Due Diligence offer is often referred to as a Letter of Intent.

The following factors should be considered in evaluation of each final binding offer:

Price

Ideally expressed as enterprise value, together with amendments to enterprise value to arrive at the proposed purchase price for the equity and any loan accounts being sold.

Completion process

Acceptability of process to completion as proposed in the Process Letter 2.

Financing

Requirements to finance offer, with any supporting guarantees/ letters of support from finance institutions. Ideally any additional processes required by financiers should be minimal.

Approvals required and ability to close the transaction

Any investment committee/ board approval and shareholder approvals still required should be considered in the evaluation

Further due diligence required

Ideally the Due Diligence should be complete, and this would typically be a requirement set out in the Process Letter 2, however there may be a requirement for some confirmatory Due Diligence, and access to a Red Data Room. These may have been requirements imposed by the vendor. Any additional timing and risks associated with any additional procedures imposed by the bidders should be evaluated with caution.

Competition Law/ Antitrust approvals required

Typically, by this stage of the process, when dealing with competitors who are potential acquirers, the vendor should, through their legal advisors, have established a view on the acceptability of the bidder from a competition law perspective. Process Letter 2 often requests the bidders view and may also request further information in support of the offer. This information be evaluated and carefully considered to avoid the selection of a final bidder who is subsequently rejected by the competition law authorities.

Evaluation of SPA mark-up

Analysis of proposed warranties, indemnities, and other proposed contractual provisions should be considered. Extensive mark-ups may not be acceptable and should be considered in the evaluation

Care should be taken not to accept an offer that is simply too good to be true. For example, an offer which has no legal mark-ups or is incomplete should be treated with caution as it may be indicative of a bidder having not properly completed their Due Diligence properly, or who may not be able to complete the transaction, nor finalize the approvals and/ or financing to complete the transaction.

Retaining multiple bidders and re-engaging with bidding parties

It is generally advised that at this stage only one bidder is selected, however there may be certain aspects of a final bid which needs to be finalized, this may relate to confirmatory Due Diligence procedures. It may be possible, albeit for only a short period of time that a particular preferred bidder is approached and asked to update / finalize their offer and given an additional short period of time to complete these procedures. Provided this time period is relatively short (say, less than a week) then it may be able to buy time with other bidders to allow the preferred bidder/s time to finalize and update their offers. Where there are bidders with close bids, there may be an opportunity to give bidders the chance to increase their price.

Once an offer has been selected, the vendor should advise the non-successful parties, and engage with the preferred bidder on an exclusive basis. This is often when sellers are most exposed, so every effort should be made to expedite the completion and signature of the SPA within the shortest possible time frame. The rejected bidders should be advised that their offer will be reconsidered if final negotiations with the single preferred bidder is not successful.

Final negotiations

Typically, final negotiations are attended by representatives of the seller, the legal advisor and the financial advisor. At times it may be appropriate for legal advisors, and the financial advisors to be involved in aspects of the negotiations and the completion of the SPA, without the involvement of the principal, but care should be taken to ensure there is frequent feedback and input with the principle. There should also be a clear negotiation mandate by the principle to his advisors. Failure to do this can result in frustrations and delays down the line.

Post completion procedures

On signature there is typically a celebration, and a sense of relief following a long and often arduous process. However, there are usually a number of Conditions Precedent which need to be completed. The financial advisor together with the legal advisor, should ensure these activities are monitored and followed up. Normally be the legal advisor prepares a completion schedule which is used as a tool to ensure these activities are all completed timeously. These activities can include shareholder approval, board and investment committee approval, release from guarantees, competition approval, finalization of financing arrangements, filing of statutory documents (For example amendment of the company constitution), signature of ancillary legal documents (e.g. shareholder agreements), and so on.

In addition to the Conditions Precedent where the agreement is subject to price adjustments through completion accounts, the financial advisor should co-ordinate this process to ensure completion thereof.

10. Legal considerations

This book is certainly not expected to be a legal reference, but an understanding of key legal considerations is important for the purposes of completing any business disposal. Whilst not in any way a substitute for legal advice, this chapter sets out a basic understanding of legal considerations in the M&A process.

SPA considerations

The process of negotiating and concluding the legal agreements and related transaction documentation can be complex and time consuming. The use of appropriate legal advice is critical and would typically require appointment of external legal counsel, with specific M&A experience, even if there is competent internal counsel.

The lead advisor on the M&A process will be expected to provide assistance and guidance, often being involved in briefing external counsel, and in providing advice around the commercial aspects of the agreements, including financial considerations such as the completion mechanism (locked box or completion accounts – see page 109).

Types of legal documents to be negotiated

In addition to a Sale and Purchase Agreement (SPA), which stipulates the terms and conditions of the sale, there may be a number of ancillary agreements/ documents which need to be negotiated concurrently, including:
- Shareholders Agreement – this is particularly relevant where the purchase if for less than 100% of the shares;
- Funding Agreements – relevant where the acquisition is via a especial purpose vehicle which is financing the acquisition with debt, or where the acquisition finance is a Condition Precedent in the SPA;
- Company constitutional documentation – often as a result if a transaction the constitution of the company needs to be amended and this requires the adoption of new corporate constitutional documentation;
- Resolutions evidencing approval by the buyer and/ or the seller;
- In the case of companies with many shareholders, and in particular public listed companies, there may be a requirement for the buyer to draft a circular to shareholders convening a meeting to approve the transaction. This is dependent on the materiality/ significance of the transaction, and the regulatory requirements of the stock exchange where the buyer/ seller is listed, and
- Release from guarantees and sureties where the seller has provided these to commercial bankers and/ or suppliers for the benefit of the target company.

The nature, extent and complexity of the legal documentation is influenced by the stake involved, with fewer legal agreements being required for a 100% disposal (For example no shareholder agreement required). Also, the nature of the legal agreements changes depending on whether to sale is an asset deal, i.e. sale of underlying business assets and transfer of liabilities, or whether the sale is for shares and shareholder loan accounts. In the event of an asset deal, significantly more ancillary schedules will be required to clearly identify the assets and liabilities which constitute the business being sold.

Components of a Sale and Purchase Agreement

The key components of a SPA include:
- **Definitions;**
- **Agreement as to what is being sold:** Typically, assets and liabilities or shares and loan accounts, depending on whether the deal is a share transaction or an asset transaction;
- **Consideration:** The purchase price as well as adjustments thereto. Particularly where there is a locked box completion mechanism, it is likely the purchase price will be adjusted for interest accrued to the seller from the Locked Box Date. In the case where completion accounts are prepared, interest will typically only accrue from the completion accounts date;
- **Conditions Precedent:** Specific conditions or events that must be in place, or come to pass, before the agreement can be binding and of effect;
- **Vendor undertakings:** clauses setting out, inter alia, how the vendor manages the business between signature date and completion;
- **MAC Clause:** Material Adverse Change clause, a clause dealing with the implications of any material adverse changes to the business which may occur during the period between signature and completion;

- **Actions on completion:** Clauses setting out what is to take place to give effect to the closing of the transaction. Typically, this would include handing over of share certificates, and the resignations of the directors;
- **Warranties:** A statement in the SPA whereby the vendor confirms facts to be true (For example the creditors listing is complete);
- **Restrictive covenants**, including non-complete clauses sometimes imposed on the seller;
- **Boilerplate clauses** such as confidentiality, entire agreement, notices, assignment, governing law, and jurisdiction;
- **Schedules supporting the agreement:** – sometimes specific warranties are schedules to the agreement, completion accounts, ancillary agreements, etc.

Asset versus Share Purchase

Where a transaction involves the sale of a target which is a company, it is typically preferable from a sellers' perspective to sell the shares rather than the assets. This results in a cleaner separation, with all assets and liabilities of the company passing with the transaction (subject to any contractual warranties and indemnities).

Under a sale of assets, only those assets specifically identified by the SPA are sold, and only liabilities specifically identified are assumed. This requires a thorough evaluation of all assets and liabilities. When a business being sold is an unincorporated division, this is often the only way to affect a sale. From a buyers' perspective, where debt is being used to finance the acquisition, as asset deal is often preferable. The reason for this is that interest is typically not deductible against the purchase of shares, whilst interest is deductible when purchasing operating assets which will produce taxable income. In addition, any company liabilities not specified and/or unknown at the date of the transaction (including historic tax liabilities) are not included in the sale, reducing risk for the buyer.

Completion mechanism

The completion mechanism is an important part of the SPA, and the lead advisor is typically called on to provide input into this. Completion mechanisms are discussed on page 108.

Warranties and Indemnities

The sale of a business comes with risk and rewards. In order to mitigate risk, purchasers will seek to allocate some of this risk back to the vendor by seeking warranties at completion. Warranties are typically statements of fact the vendor represents to be true (for example that all tax liabilities have been quantified and brought to account). The process of disclosure by the seller is how the seller limits his liability as disclosure of information eliminates the effect of the warranty (for example, the disclosure of the details of a dispute with the tax authorities). In addition to this, caps, baskets, *de minimus* limits, and time period restrictions are all used to limit potential claims the purchaser may have in relation to warranties.

An indemnity represents a better protection for the buyer in that regardless of disclosure, any loss resulting in relation from an identification, is reimbursed by the vendor. One is not able to disclose facts to limit liability against an indemnity.

Conditions Precedent and Post signature activities

Most SPAs include a number of suspensive conditions or Conditions Precedent. These represent conditions which need to be met for an agreement to be effective. Typically, a time frame is provided for the meeting of the condition, failing which the agreement will become null and void. Some of these Conditions Precedent relate to events outside of the control of the buyer and seller, whilst other need to be performed by the buyer and/ or seller before the agreement becomes effective. Examples of typical Conditions Precedent include:
- Approval by board of seller;
- Approval by board of buyer;
- Filing of resolutions with statutory bodies;
- Filing of amendments to the company's constitution;
- Release of the seller from guarantees provided in respect of the target;
- Agreement for the cession/ assignment of material contracts and/ or the receipt of consent where major contracts include change in control clauses; and
- Approval by certain regulatory bodies (Competition regulators, banking regulators, exchange control authorities, etc.).

Conditions Precedent are usually subject to achievement by a dead-end date, after which the agreement is null and void, regardless of whether the conditions are met. It is therefore important that a proper action plan is agreed, to ensure all the conditions are completed within the stipulated time frame. This timetable should be driven by the advisors in consultation with the legal advisors.

Warranty and indemnity insurance

In a typical M&A transaction, a buyer seeks protection to reduce its risk by seeking warranties and indemnities from the seller. Warranties are generally mitigated by the seller by disclosing of facts and circumstances (through the data room, Q&A process, and a disclosure letter) to the seller.

Where financial investors (private equity firms) are sellers, they are sometimes restricted in terms of the warranties that can be provided. Typically, independent private equity funds have a fixed life and are liquidated and the end of life, with funds being distributed to investors. Accordingly, there often can be no recourse to buyers should they wish to claim against the warranties. This can be alleviated by the provision of cash to be placed in escrow, however this is not attractive to financial sellers as it typically ties up capital beyond the fund life.

Similar proposals are often evident when dealing with the sale of the assets of a trust which is to be liquidated, or the sale of a public listed company which will result in the proceeds being distributed to a diverse range of public shareholders without any ability to claim recourse.

In order to manage these situations, achieve liquidity for the sellers, provide the required comfort to the buyer and avoid deadlock situations, the provision of Warranty and Indemnity Insurance (W&I Insurance) has developed to facilitate clean exits and avoid the need to place any of the seller's proceeds in escrow.

Use of W&I insurance in a sale process

It is now common that W&I insurance is structured into a sale process by the sellers and its advisors. A broker is typically engaged fairly early in the process and works with the seller to structure a W&I Policy. This would usually involve sharing of the Information Memorandum, other marketing information, process letters, etc. under confidentiality, and the initial data room with the broker who would then procure quotes from insurers. The W&I Insurance broker can then solicit competitive quotes from insurers with a view to selecting a preferred insurer based on indicative quotes.

The high-level terms and the proposed quote is typically then made available for disclosure into the data room for the benefit of prospective bidders.

These high-level terms would be based on a limited review of the transaction material by the prospective insurer and would be subject to an underwriting review by the insurer. Thus, the terms disclosed are normally a preliminary quote.

Buyers vs seller's insurance

Typically, it would be preferable for the seller to facilitate the insurer to obtain a buyer-side insurance policy. In this manner the cost of the insurance premium can be borne by the buyer.

This can be facilitated by the seller, who can obtains quotes, and select a preferred insurer. The relationship between the underwriter then flips over, much like would happen if a buyer was to solicit quotes for stapled finance. The policy is ultimately entered directly between the final buyer and the insurer.

The cover under a seller-side policy covers the buyer against the sellers' representations (innocent or otherwise) and the buyer claims directly against the insurance policy. In a policy entered into between the seller and the underwriter (a seller side policy), the policy covers the seller, but only for its own innocent misrepresentations (i.e. Fraud by the seller is excluded from the policy).

Underwriting process

The underwriting process is typically non-intrusive and under a buyer-side policy, entails a review of the buyer's due diligence reports and process. This will include a review of the final SPA, the bidders' due diligence reports, the data room index and contents, the preferred bidders Q&A register, and would typically include a discussion with the buyers deal team and external advisors. This process can take about one week.

This underwriting process requires the incurrence of expenses by the insurer, and insurers will sometimes require an underwriting fee to defray this expense, in the event that the policy is not taken up (for example, if the CP's are not met).

Premiums are generally between 1% and 3% of the cover purchased and are influenced by factors such as the industry sector, geographical jurisdiction of the target, as well as the quality of the transaction process and the advisors.

Typically, the broad coverage supplied by the policy matches the representations and warranties in the SPA as closely as possible.

Claims

Claims are generally subject to a retention or excess which is typically set at 1% of the value of the transaction.

Glossary of M&A Terminology

Buyer Universe	See Long List;
Captive Fund	A Private Equity Fund created for the benefit of a single entity/parent or family office. These funds are often open ended;
Carried Interest	The remuneration of a Private Equity Fund manager usually includes a percentage of the added value that the fund realizes for its investors. The percentage is usually paid after the investors have realized a specific benchmark return (or Hurdle Rate). The fund manager's share in the return above the hurdle rate is called the carried interest;
Carve Out	A process of determining a stand-alone set of financial statements for a particular business. It is usually prepared when there is no separate accounting for a division which is being sold;

Closed Ended Funds	Typical private equity fund structure, whereby funds are raised from third-party investors. At a point these funds are typically closed to further investments and have a defined duration/ fund life;
Completion Accounts	Financial Statements prepared for the purpose of determining the final purchase process to be paid for a business;
Conditions Precedent	A condition must occur subsequent to the signing of a SPA for the agreement to be binding. A typical example of a Condition Precedent is obtaining approval for the acquisition from the competition authorities;
Confidentiality Agreement	See Non-Disclosure Agreement;
Confirmatory Due Diligence	A limited scope Due Diligence preformed after the conclusion of a preliminary Due Diligence. As the name suggests, the scope is limited to confirming certain key aspects of the preliminary Due Diligence. A Confirmatory Due Diligence often be completed on top of/ in addition to a Vendor Due Diligence;

Data Book	A report commissioned by the seller for the purpose of providing prospective bidders with information about the target business. It is similar to a Financial Due Diligence, except that it does not include recommendations and conclusions, and it more factual in nature. It is therefore something which a prospective bidder should not rely on, and cannot be seen as a substitute for a due diligence;
DCF	Discounted Cash Flow, a valuation methodology based on the discounting of all future free cash flows which accrue to the owners of a firm;
Due Diligence	In investigation into a target performed by investors and/ or their advisors prior to the making of an investment decision. The Due Diligence often comprises of a Financial Due Diligence, Tax Due Diligence, and Legal Due Diligence;
EBITDA	Earnings Before Interest, Tax, Depreciation and Amortization. This is a measure of the operating cash flow earnings of a firm before interest, tax and any cash flow effects of changes in working capital and investments in capital expenditure;

Enterprise Value	The value of a firm as attributable to all provides of capital. Importantly it therefore represents the value of a business before the deduction of the value of debts outstanding;
Equity Check	In relation to an acquisition, the equity check represents that proportion of the acquisition funding provided by the acquirer, i.e. it excludes that portion of the purchase prices which is funded by third parties, including debt and mezzanine finance
Final Offer	The final offer provided by the seller, usually accompanied by a mark-up of the draft SPA
Financial Buyer	A buyer who is typically not a strategic buyer, and is not looking to extract operational synergies though an acquisition, and would typically not have extensive operational expertise in the same sector as the target. A typical financial buyer would include private equity investors. Financial Buyers usually apply debt when making an acquisition;

Financial Due Diligence	The review of the historical and future figures of a target business. The focus in this context is often on the quality of earnings (how robust are the historical results?), the quality of net debt (which items could all be taken into consideration in determining the net financial debt, the forecast (analysis of the budgets and future projections) and the normalized working capital;
First Right of Refusal	A contractual right that gives its holder the option to enter a business transaction with the owner of a business, according to specified terms, before the owner is entitled to enter into that transaction with a third party;
General Partner	In order to maintain the limitations in liability as a limited partnership, a fund must also have a general partner who has unlimited liability. The general partner is associated with the management company of the investment fund;
Hurdle Rate	The return that a fund must realize on an investment for its investors before the fund manager can share in any Carried Interest.
IM	See Information Memorandum;

Information Memorandum	The Information Memorandum is a document that describes a target company. The Information Memorandum is typically sent to potential buyers after the signing of an NDA, and is usually accompanied by a Process Letter.
Lehman Formula	A formula for the determination of the sellers' advisors fee. The fee works on a progressively descending scale such that at lower thresholds, a higher percentage is charged, but above progressive thresholds, the incremental fee is calculated with reference to a lower percentage;
Limited Partner	Anglo-Saxon funds are often set up as tax transparent limited partnerships with limited liability for the investors (the limited partners). The Limited Partners provide the majority of the capital for the Private Equity Fund, and are generally not involved in the management of the fund. These limited partnerships are often offshore partnerships for maximum legal flexibility.

Locked Box	A locked box mechanism is a methodology to determine the purchase price of the shares in a company with reference to a historical balance sheet, rather than closing accounts, which would only be prepared on completion of the conditions precedent. It is contractually agreed that there cannot be any cash flowing out of the company (the locked box) in the form of the payment of dividends or management fees. All other cash movements remain within the company and are thus assumed to have no effect on value. This method can only be applied if the buyer can obtain a very good picture of the balance sheet of the company during the acquisition;
Locked Box Accounts	Referenced accounts for the purpose of determining the purchase price where a Locked Box mechanism is applied;
Locked Box Date Accounts are prepared;	The date at which the Locked Box

Locked Box Letter	A letter to supplement Process Letter 2, and often accompanying the draft SPA, setting out the sellers proposed basis for the determination of the reconciliation of Enterprise Value to Equity Value, as well as the proposed rate of interest to apply between the Locked Box Date and the date when the agreement becomes effective and the purchase price is paid;
Long List	The initial long list – sometimes referred to as the Buyer Universe – of potential buyers for a target. This long list is so-called as it is prior to the identification of parties who will be approached with a Teaser;
NAV	Net Asset Value, being the accounting value of assets, less the accounting value of liabilities;
NDA	Non-disclosure Agreement
Pre-emptive rights	A clause in an option, security or merger agreement that gives the investor the right to maintain his or her percentage ownership of a company by buying a proportionate number of shares of any future issue of the security;

Private Equity Fund	A fund created for investment in businesses, these can be closed ended or open-ended funds;
Process Letter 1	The first process letter (Process Letter 1) is issued to parties approached who sign the NDA. It contains information on how the seller proposes to manage the sale process, by which date a Non-binding Indicative Offer is expected and what requirements it must meet, and how the next phase will look thereafter;
Process Letter 2	Process Letter 2 is issued to those bidders whose Non-Binding Indicative Offers are acceptable, and who have been selected to participate in the Due Diligence phase of the disposal process. The letter sets out how the Due Diligence process will be managed, how Final Offers will be assessed, and the date which they are due;
Profit Warranty	A predetermined future level of profits, which links to the level of a deferred payment to be made by the buyer to the seller;

Red Data Room	A data room reserved only for a single preferred/ final bidder. It contains particularly sensitive information which is not divulged through the data room;
ROE	Return on Equity;
Short List	The short list of companies that will be contacted in an initial phase to gauge their interest. The short list is often created after making a selection from the Long List;
Shortlisted Bidder	Prospective buyer of a target business, typically shortlisted for Due Diligence after the submission of a Non-Binding Indicative-Offer which is deemed acceptable;
SPA	Sale and Purchase Agreement, the agreement evidencing the terms and conditions for the sale of shares or the sale of the underlying assets and liabilities of a business;
SWOT analysis	A strategic analysis of the Strengths, Weaknesses Opportunities and Threats in a business;

Teaser	The anonymous profile of the company that is sent to potential buyers. The aim is to determine whether such a purchase could interest them without the identity of the company being disclosed;
Top-up Due Diligence	Additional Due Diligence procedures performed by a buyer, over and above that performed in the Vendor Due Diligence
Trade Buyer	Unlike a Financial Buyer, a Trade Buyer is typically motivated by the ability to extract operational synergies of an acquisition or to expand an existing market through acquiring a business in the same sector, but in a different geography. They are therefore motivated by strategic considerations, and are sometimes also referred to as 'strategic buyers';
VDD	Vendor Due Diligence;
Vendor	The seller of a business;
Vendor Due diligence	A Due Diligence that is commissioned by a seller for the benefit pf prospective bidders;

Vendor Loan	A loan, or deferred payment mechanism provided by the seller of the business to allow for the payment of the purchase price, or a portion thereof, over a period of time;
Virtual Data Room	A data room hosted on remote server containing information made available to prospective bidders for the purpose of their Due Diligence;
WACC	Weighted Average Cost of Capital, the rate applied to discount future free cash flows in order to arrive at the Enterprise Value of a firm.

Annexure: Data Room Checklist

Courtesy of KPMG in South Africa. This checklist is purely indicative and will have to be tailored for particular circumstances and jurisdiction.

CORPORATE INFORMATION

General corporate information

1 Company history and background
2 Certificates of incorporation and any certificates of incorporation on change of name for each of the companies in the group (the "Group")
3 Current memorandum and articles of association of each Group company
4 Details of the authorized and issued share capital and any loan capital of each Group company
5 Schedule of issuances, sale and repurchases of shares or other securities since inception
6 Corporate organization chart showing subsidiaries and subsidiary undertakings of the Group, joint ventures, investments, associate companies and partnerships
7 Details of major shareholders by class of share, number of shares beneficially owned, purchase price of shares, date of purchase, voting rights and outstanding options

8. Details of any change in the interest of any Group company in any undertaking within the last three years
9. Details of any agreement or commitment to allot, issue or transfer any shares or debentures or securities of any Group company
10. Details of any rights of pre-emption or restriction on transfer relating to any shares
11. Copies of agreements relating to shareholder agreements, voting agreements and irrevocable proxies, and other restrictions on share transfers
12. Details of any branch, agency, place of business or permanent establishment of the Group
13. Full names and addresses of each director, officer, secretary and auditor of the Group
14. Job profile and summary CV of key management staff
15. Minutes of Meetings of Management and Directors
16. Copy of detailed business plan and strategy (short, medium and long-term) for the Group and for each division, including income statement forecasts for the next three years
17. List of associations and organizations the Group belongs to
18. Documents relating to recent company acquisitions over the past five years, including companies and other business entities, properties, major plant and equipment and operations
19. Documents relating to recent company divestitures over the past five years, including companies and other business entities, properties, major plant and equipment and operations

FINANCIAL INFORMATION

Borrowings

1. Details and copies of all overdraft, loan or other financial facilities (including foreign exchange facilities) to which any member of the Group is a party, and the amounts outstanding under those facilities
2. Copies of credit agreements, loan agreements, notes, debentures, capital leases, security agreements and pledges relating to financing transactions, agreements regarding sales of accounts receivable and other agreements
3. Copies of all debentures, charges, guarantees, indemnities and other security given to secure the facilities referred to in 1 above
4. Details of any borrowings made by the Group since last reporting date

Working capital

5. The Group profit and cash forecasts or budgets for the current year and (if any) any subsequent years for which projections have been prepared
6. Details of estimated future funding requirements
7. Cash, inventory and working capital requirements for the past two years and normal requirements based on trade practices, credit terms to customer and inventory levels maintained

Working capital management

8   Bank and overdraft facilities
9   Analysis of cash/bank balances and reconciliation to bank position
10 Cash flow statement (past 3 years plus forecast)
11 Debtors, creditors and inventory days in the past and forecast

Capital expenditure

12 Details of planned and committed capital expenditure, split by maintenance and expansionary (including store roll-outs)

Insolvency

13 Details of any order, petition or resolution for the winding up of any member of the Group
14 Details of any administration order made or administrator appointed or any step taken or procedure commenced with a view to the appointment of an administrator in respect of any member of the Group
15 Details of any receiver or administrative receiver appointed in respect of any member of the Group or all or any of its assets
16 Details of any unsatisfied judgment outstanding against any member of the Group

17 Details of any composition or similar arrangement with creditors including but not limited to a voluntary arrangement in respect of any member of the Group
18 Details of any moratorium in force or any step taken, or procedure commenced with a view to entering into such a moratorium in respect of any member of the Group

ACCOUNTING INFORMATION

Accounts

1 The latest audited annual financial statements of all the Group companies and the consolidation working papers for the last five years
2 List of the Group's accounting policies and any recent changes and the impact thereof
3 Copies of the monthly management accounts of the Group for the current financial year
4 Copies of all financial budgets, forecasts and projections (showing underlying assumptions) prepared by or for senior management in the last three years
5 Details of any contingent assets and liabilities or off-balance sheet items not included in the accounts referred to in 1
6 Copies of all auditors' management letters and management's representation letters to the auditors in respect of the accounts referred to in 1
7 The reports/results of internal audits of the Company for the past 3 years

Historic profitability analysis

8. Provide the monthly management accounts for the last two financial year ends and year to date
9. Provide details of the key revenue drivers and key performance indicators
10. Provide list of major customers with associated sales activity (including intra-group)
11. Provide a listing of sales (both units and value) and gross margins (product profitability) by significant customers and major product lines
12. Provide details of cost of sales and purchases by customer and product.
13. Provide a detailed listing of general and administrative expenses (if in management accounts ignore)

Projections

14. Provide projection methodology and assumptions
15. Provide management's financial models and underlying projected costs and revenue forecast assumptions
16. Provide details of any special features currently influencing trading performance, including exceptional income and costs.
17. Provide details of working capital assumptions
18. Provide income statement and cash flow statement actual versus budgeted performance for the past three years and year to date results (if not in the management accounts)

Events since last reporting date

19 Details of any capital asset of a value in excess of $[☐] which has been acquired or disposed of (or agreed to be acquired or disposed of) since last reporting date and any contract entered into since last reporting date involving capital expenditure in excess of $[☐]
20 Details of any change in the accounting reference period of any member of the Group made since last reporting date
21 Details of any book debt shown in the accounts which has not been realized for the sum shown therein and any indication received that any book debts shown in the accounts are bad or doubtful
22 Details of any unusual increase or decrease in trading stock levels since last reporting date
23 Details of any price reductions, discounts or allowances on sales of trading stock or services offered by the any member of the Group since last reporting date
24 Details of any material contracts entered into since last reporting date

Balance sheet

25 Provide trial balances at respective period ends
26 Property, plant and equipment
27 Provide details of any tangible fixed asset valuations
28 Provide details as to the existence of idle, underutilized or impaired assets
29 Provide details of any significant fixed asset purchase commitments and any other planned capital expenditure projects
30 Provide details of capital expenditures by type (maintenance, expansion, new product/process)

31 Schedule of capital and revenue commitments (distinguishing between authorized and contracted commitments)

Accounts receivable

32 Provide details of all categories (reconciliation) which make up the balance of accounts receivable in the financial statements
33 Provide details on the methodology of the doubtful debts provisioning.
34 Provide a listing of all bad debts written off for the periods under review.
35 Provide a listing of debtors identified as potentially bad
36 Provide details of sales returns and credit notes over the periods under review.
37 Brief description of any trading arrangements within the Group, including any services provided by group head office, together with copies of any written agreements recording such arrangements and details of the current amounts outstanding between the Group companies in respect of such arrangements
38 Description of bad debt policy, credit policy and collection procedures
39 The accounts receivable ageing reports of the Group for the past 2 years for the month of [☐]
40 Brief description of any trading arrangements within the Group, including any services provided by group head office, together with copies of any written agreements recording such arrangements and details of the current amounts outstanding between the Group companies in respect of such arrangements
41 Description of bad debt policy, credit policy and collection procedures

Inventory

41. Inventories (per division):-
    - Location, including consigned goods;
    - Finished goods by product;
    - Raw materials by product;
    - Work-in-progress by product;
    - Accounting procedures and practices;
    - Pricing methods; and
    - Provisions for obsolete or slow-moving stock

Accounts payable, accrued liabilities and provisions

42. Schedule of all accounts payable accrued liabilities and provisions
43. Provide the accounts payable aged trial balance
44. Provide details of account payable terms, payment practices and cut-off procedures
45. Provide a summary of other accounts payable, accrued and current

Intercompany and related party transactions

46. Provide details on sales to related parties, intercompany sales and service arrangements, transfer pricing policies, services provided by/to related party etc.

CONTRACTUAL AND TRADING INFORMATION

References to "material" contracts, agreements etc. are to contracts or agreements which involve revenues and/or expenditure of the Group in excess of $[□] per annum (either in any one financial year or on average) and which, individually, are of material commercial importance to the operation of the Group.

Contracts and commitments

1. Copies of any material outstanding guarantee, indemnity, surety relationship or letter of credit provided by any member of the Group to a third party
2. Copies of all material sales representative, agent and dealer agreements
3. Copies of any material management agreements
4. Copies of material distribution agreements
5. Copies of material licenses agreements
6. Copies of any contract for rent, lease, hire, hire purchase, credit sale, conditional sale or purchase by instalments calling for payments aggregating, in any 12 month period, $[□] (or the equivalent in any other currency) or more
7. Copies of any material contracts with any intermediaries, e.g. consultants or independent sales agents
8. Copies of all material fiduciary and agency agreements

9 Copies of any material sub-contracting arrangements
10 Copies of any material supply and customer agreements
11 Copies of any material contracts with government entities
12 Copies of any material research and development/collaboration agreements
13 Copies of any joint venture agreement or arrangement, partnership rights or obligations to which a member of the Group is a party
14 Copies of any material contract or arrangement in which any director of a member of the Group, or a person connected with a director, has an interest
15 Copies of material membership agreements or affiliations with trade associations and any rules/codes of conduct applicable thereto
16 Copies of any agreement or contract which is of three years' or greater duration
17 Copies of any material loss-making contracts
18 Copies of all material agreements which cannot be terminated by a member of the Group on three months' notice or less without payment of compensation or any special fees
19 Copies of any material contract or arrangement (including those with the directors, management and employees) which can be terminated in the event of any change in the underlying ownership or control of the Group or would be materially affected by such change
20 Copies of any current standard terms of business
21 Details of any outstanding bid or tender or sale or service proposal which is material in relation to the Group's business or which, if accepted, would be likely to result in a loss
22 Copies of all commitments entered into for (i) new buildings, (ii) machinery, (iii) stock and (iv) any other matters aggregating, in any twelve month period, $[☐] (or the equivalent in any other currency) or more

23 Copies of outstanding powers of attorney/authorization letters authorizing signing of bids, purchase orders and contracts generally
24 Standard forms of warranties, quotations, purchase orders and invoices
25 Schedules of royalty payment obligations and of royalties paid and accrued by license and product.
26 Copies of agreements with brokers, investment bankers or finders relating to any transaction or proposed transaction since inception

Trading

27. Details of any material customer or supplier which during the last twelve months has ceased or indicated an intention to cease trading or substantially reduce its trading with the Group
28. Details of any person or persons together who have purchased from or sold to the Group more than 10 per cent of the aggregate amount of all sales or purchases made by the Group in the last or current financial year
29. Details of any other person or persons together on whom the Group is materially dependent or the cessation of transactions with whom would materially affect the business of the Group Insurance
30. Copies of all insurance contracts and policy documents (plus a schedule showing insurance cover by policy) and details of all outstanding material claims and material claims made by or paid to the Group in the last three years
31. Details of directors and officers liability insurance policies

INDUSTRY ANALYSIS

Market share

1. Market share per key product category by volume and value
2. Market share per key product category by volume and value for major competitor products
3. Market share per key product category by volume and value
4. Growth per key product category
5. Historic growth per key product category for the past 3 years
6. Forecast growth per key product category for the next 3 years

CUSTOMERS AND SALES

Customer Environment

1. Contribution of key channels and/or customers to total market
2. Contribution of key channels and/or customers to the company

3. Number of Customers serviced directly by the company – preferably by channel and region
4. Growth in number of customers serviced directly by the company over the last 5 years
5. List any large multi-national or local retailers and wholesalers

Market Position

6. Company, Category and Brand market shares currently and the trended market share performance over the last 5 years for total market, channels and key customers if available
7. Competitors' market shares currently and trended market share performance over the past 5 years for total market and key channels
8. A perspective of the nature of relationships between the company and its key customers

Route to Market

9. Overview of the route to market used to get product to outlets within the different channels, including use of the company's own vehicles as well as third party distributors
10. Overview of competitors' routes to market
11. List of any distribution centres owned and run by customers

Operations

12. Organogram of all structures within the customer division, including people employed by the company as well as contracted agents
13. Detail regarding payment of customer managers and staff – i.e. fixed cost, commission structures etc.
14. Overview of key measures used to manage the customer team and sales force
15. Detail regarding the sales information system available, as well as example of the types of reports being used
16. Detail with regards to any training that has been conducted over the last 2 years, as well as any areas that require training
17. Detail regarding external market information providers such as Nielsen
18. An explanation of what role the customer function plays in new product development

Financial Performance

19. Name the 10 largest customers and/or channels in terms of contribution to the company's sales and show how their contribution has increased or decreased over the past 5 years (volume and value)
20. Detail the actual sales (volume and value) to these top 10 customers over the past 3 years
21. Average $/volume measure realization over the past 3 years
22. Cost of doing business with customers – discounts, rebates, promotional monies, any other – current position as well as trends over the last 3 years

23. A model income statement showing the actual costs attributed to customer, as well as where in the income statement these costs are allocated

OPERATIONS

Sales and marketing

1. Details of the marketing and promotional plans per key product category
2. Description of the sales policies, key trading terms per major customer and standard terms of supply
3. Overview of the Group's new product development methodology
4. Details of the Group's product and pricing strategies per key product category and major customer
5. List of the sales volumes and value for the top five suppliers by key product by category for the past three years and forecast for the next three years
6. List of selling and marketing costs by key product by category by customer for the past three years and forecast for the next three years
7. Copies of any consumer research performed at the request of the Group
8. Sales reports by sales representative, both in-house and intermediaries, for the past three years
9. Projected market size of participating brands in defined categories and geographic coverage

10. Details of the marketing and promotional plans per key product category, as well as historic spend on marketing and budgeting spend by category
11. Details of the Group's product and pricing strategies per key product category and major customer including pricing elasticity
12. List of selling and marketing costs by key product by category by customer for the past three years and forecast for the next three years
13. Channel and customer strategy - past, present and future
14. Provide a consumer analysis by major brand including:
    - Level of brand loyalty
    - Consumer satisfaction for seller versus competitor's products
    - Product and portfolio positioning
    - All consumer research
    - Consumer complaints and trends
15. Market segmentation of product and brand offering
16. Who are the Company's competitors? What is the Company's relative market share?
17. Competitor analysis: Key brand performance versus the competition in terms of price, positioning, margins, distribution channels and other relevant financial and qualitative comparisons. Any other competitor strategy/insights as understood.
18. What are potential competitive threats in the future; innovation?
19. Have any of the Company's competitors recently changed their tactics with regards to how they market their products (i.e., offering new services, teaming with other vendors, shifting distribution channels)?

Procurement

20. Description of the Group's procurement and tender policies, processes and standard terms of purchase
21. List of the purchase volumes and value for the top five suppliers by key product by category for the past three years and forecast for the next three years
22. Details of imported versus locally sourced raw materials and finished goods over the past three years
23. List of Suppliers
    - By major raw materials
    - By volume and value
    - Understand if there are any specific dependencies
    - Is it possible to rationalize the list
    - Can we use Client current suppliers and obtain materials at a better price
24. Procurement Policies and Procedures
    - Overview
    - Tender process
    - Adherence levels
    - Are they adequate?
    - Quality Controls relating to final selection of supplier
25. Availability
    - What is the lead time between order and delivery?
    - Are there any scarce resources
26. Analysis of Imported Material
    - Lead time between order and delivery
    - Volume and price per unit of imported material
    - Is it possible to source locally?
    - Historic pricing and delivery issues
    - Major suppliers and alternative international suppliers, are there any major dependencies

27. Pricing of raw materials
    - Can we obtain at a better price?
    - Any regulations on pricing of materials
    - How often is this negotiated?
    - Impact of Client Acquisition on buying power, do we foresee any savings
28. Contracts with suppliers
    - Are there SLA's in place with all major suppliers?
    - Are there strict quality control aspects built into the SLA
29. Details of consignment materials on hand:
    - Is there a valid agreement in place?
    - What are the terms?
    - Usage analysis
30. Seasonality Impact Analysis
31. Analyze competition for sources of supply
32. Trend Analysis

Manufacturing / capacity

33. Description of production processes and systems by product, including equipment and machinery utilized
34. Layout of the manufacturing facilities
35. Details of manufacturing capacity by month by production line over the past three years
36. Description of the Group's quality control systems
37. Maintenances costs and schedules over the past three years
38. Manufacturing expenses by type per product per category over the past three years
39. Details of any contract manufacturing over the past three years
40. Detailed Analysis of:

- Production method by line
- Facilities
- Efficiency
- Equipment
- General condition
- Review of any planned shut downs
- Upgrades or replacements required and cost implications
- New Tech or Old Tech and the implications thereof
- Layout
- Quality Control Systems

41. Manufacturing Capacity by line
    - Overview
    - Maximum capacity
    - Current average
    - Peak Seasonal average
    - Is the capacity sufficient – cost implications to improve capacity if necessary

42. Bolt on Implications
    - Can synergies be realized from bolting on Client products on the sellers line or bolting on sellers products on Client's production line
    - Conversion cost and other related costs of Bolt On
    - Annual savings going forward
    - Capacity issues if any after Bolt On

43. Manufacturing expenses and cost structures
    - Review by product
    - Identification of issues and savings

44. Raw material handling
    - Volumes
    - Storage Capacity
    - Hazardous material
    - Detailed analysis of contract manufacturing (if any)

45. Maintenance
    - Review of historic maintenances costs and schedules
    - Any immediate issues to be addressed and cost implications
    - Overview of maintenance department and assess whether any
    - Special skills required for factory maintenance
46. Production Costing by Product
    - Analysis of sellers costing methodology and accuracy assessment
    - Assessment of costing in a Bolt on Environment
    - Assessment of costing on a Stand Alone basis after Client Acquisition
47. Overview of Merger Costs
    - Detailed costing and justification of Capex required
    - Detailed costing and justification of maintenance expenditure to be incurred

Distribution

48. Brief description of the Group's usual arrangements for the transportation of goods to customers and from suppliers
49. List of warehouses where inventory, including consignments inventory, is held by region and stockholding
50. Distribution expenses by type per product per category over the past three years
51. Review of Current Agreements with transporters
    - Understand the costs
    - Assess the costs for contract cancellations

- Assess the costs to migrate to Client's transporters
- Distribution costs to warehouse
- Distribution costs to market
- Fixed Costs
- Initial Fees

52. Assess IT System Implications
    - Loading of products on to Client Systems
    - Units vs. Cases
53. Understand pallet configuration requirements for Client migration
54. Assess whether current packaging suitable for Client s transportation methods and load requirements
55. Provide a list of Warehouses where inventory is held:
    - By region and stockholding
    - Assess if any of this is consignment inventory
    - Assess the cost to migrate to the Client system
56. Understand full impact on the customer:
    - NODs and NDDs, etc.
57. Any other pertinent issues

RESEARCH & DEVELOPMENT ("R&D")

1. Description of the Group's R&D structure, systems and processes
2. Strategic, marketing and business plans and studies of current and expected R&D, including a timetable of new product launches
3. Copies of consultants', engineers' or management reports and studies related to material aspects of the Group's business operations

4. Description of any pending research and development activity
5. Description of backup, archive and disaster recovery procedures (formulae/recipes/new product development research)
6. Descriptions of the background of all technical employees together with a list of their accomplishments and a description of their current involvement with particular projects
7. Details of systems, procedures, schedules and backup materials for the development and maintenance of the software
8. Details of current "bug" lists, customer support logs, and problem reports
9. Details of future product design specifications or descriptions for any and all projects underway or anticipated, including projected dates of delivery, schedules and resource requirements
10. Have any of the Company's competitors recently changed their tactics with regards to how they market their products. For example offering new services, teaming with other vendors, shifting distribution channels
11. Details of the marketing and promotional plans per key product category, as well as historic spend on marketing and budgeting spend by category

LITIGATION AND COMPLIANCE INFORMATION

Note: Documents relating to current or potential litigation or proceedings should be limited to basic factual information which is already known to both parties to the dispute and should exclude any information or advice which is or might be subject to legal privilege.

Litigation

1. List and description of all current, pending, threatened or expected material litigation, arbitration, mediation or administrative or criminal proceedings in which the Group is or is expected to become engaged (including a copy of pleadings, interrogatories, questionnaires etc. where available) since incorporation
2. The description should include, inter alia:
    - The parties;
    - Summary of the issue; and
    - The maximum liability which the relevant Group Company might incur if an unfavourable decision is made.
3. Details of any violation or alleged violation of any law, order, ruling or regulation, or of any breach or alleged breach of any obligation or duty of any member of the Group, which might lead to an unfavourable judgment, decision, ruling or finding affecting the relevant company
4. Details of any allegation that the Group has sold or provided any product or service which does not comply with all applicable laws, regulations or standards or which is defective or dangerous or not in accordance with any representation or warranty, express or implied, given in respect of it

5. Details of any notifications of any investigation or enquiry into the affairs of the Group or requests for information from any governmental or other body
6. Copies of any prohibition notice, notice to warn or suspension notice served on the Group under Consumer Protection laws
7. Export licenses and other documents relating to the export of the Company's products
8. Other governmental permits, licenses, approvals and consents, together with related documents and correspondence, including authorisation to do business in jurisdictions outside the country and repatriation of earnings, royalties or other payments
9. Material reports filed, delivered or otherwise presented to federal, state or foreign governmental agencies or regulatory bodies since inception
10. Notices, citations, reports, letters and other communications to governmental agencies
11. Schedule of legal counsel over the last five years

Services Licenses and Intellectual Property

12. List and copies of contracts of the business including services and license agreements
13. List of contracts that may require further action and the supporting documents related to the status of the project
14. Software license, support and similar agreements, including any agreements affording third parties rights to distribute software not owned by them
15. Standard forms of software license, quotations, support and similar agreements
16. Standard forms of warranties, quotations, purchase orders and invoices

17. Secrecy, confidentiality and nondisclosure agreements with employees, developers or other third parties (please indicate any employee not covered by such agreements)
18. List of software developers and/or contractors who may have contributed to the work
19. Source code, recipe and/ or formulae listings in both hard copy and electronic format; and a list of persons having copies of, or access to source codes
20. Schedule of patents, trademarks, service marks, trade secrets, copyrights, domain names and other intangible assets, and all related applications, registrations, licenses, assignments, security agreements and ownership documents
21. All private label, joint venture, partnership, distributorship, teaming, agency, commission, brokerage, conditional sale, consulting, franchise or representative agreements to which the Company is a party
22. Copies of all issued patents and patent applications
23. Proprietary rights policies and usage guidelines, including intellectual property audits, trademark and service mark proper use rules, copyright notice and proprietary rights notice templates and usage guidelines, employee invention disclosure policies and procedures for protection, marking and use of confidential information
24. Schedules of royalty payment obligations and of royalties paid and accrued by license and product
25. Methods used for accounting for software development expenditures and software maintenance revenues
26. List, by product, of all third party and public domain intellectual property rights and technologies used in or required for developing, using, selling or copying the Company's products

27. List and description, and copies of all documents for all significant domain names, trade secrets, copyrights, patents, patents pending, proprietary designs or proprietary schematics
28. List of all restrictions/required consents relating to transfer of any assets including intellectual property rights and licenses
29. Agreements with third parties under which the Company has the right to make, use or sell products or technology, use third party trademarks, trade names, copyrighted or proprietary information or other intellectual property or which obligate the Company to pay royalties with respect to intellectual property
30. A list of each of the software programs of the Company, a description of the functions and features of each, and a chronology of their respective development
31. All records and documentation maintained by the Company documenting the development, authorship or ownership of the software programs and related technology
32. Agreements, options, or other commitments giving anyone any rights to acquire any right, title, or interest in the software programs or related technology of the Company
33. A description of the how services and software are currently marketed

Legal compliance by the company

34. Notices, citations, reports, letters and other communications to governmental agencies
35. List of pending investigations and governmental proceeding

36. Export licenses and other documents relating to the export of the Company's products
37. Other governmental permits, licenses, approvals and consents, together with related documents and correspondence, including authorization to do business in jurisdictions outside the country and repatriation of earnings, royalties or other payments
38. Material reports filed, delivered or otherwise presented to federal, state or foreign governmental agencies or regulatory bodies since inception
39. Environmental audit and inspection reports and monitoring and test reports (such as underground storage tank, groundwater, surface water, soil, sewer discharges and air emissions), whether performed internally or by third parties, and any related memoranda and correspondence

Other contracts of the company

40. Any agreement with affiliates or related parties of management or key personnel
41. Indemnification contracts and similar arrangements for officers, directors or others
42. Insurance policies, including casualty, property, liability, key man, directors and officers, and errors and omissions
43. Other contracts involving in excess of $___ whether or not entered into in the ordinary course of business, including:
    - Domestic and foreign marketing agreements, including sales agent, sales representative, dealer and distributor agreements, consignment and pricing agreements
    - Government contracts and subcontracts
    - Supply agreements

- Purchase, output and requirements contracts
- Joint venture and partnership agreements
- Agreements regarding research and development
- Management and service agreements
- Performance guarantees and bonds
- Advertising agreements.

44. Other contracts entered into outside the ordinary course of business.
45. All agreements, agreements in principle or letters of intent concerning confidentiality, non-competition, acquisition or disposition of the Company's product lines, assets or operations, mergers and the like, which might restrict the activities of the Company or its successors or assigns.

Competition and trade regulation

46. Details of any judgment, order or any other decision of any competition authority, sectoral regulator, or of any court binding on the Group
47. Details of any current or pending investigation by, or proceeding before, any competition authority, sectoral regulator, or any court, including details of any pending threat by a competition authority or sectoral regulator to open any such investigations or proceedings
48. Details of any pending threat by a third party to complain to a competition authority or sectoral regulator or to commence anti-trust proceedings
49. Details of any complaints made to a competition authority or sectoral regulator and of any anti-trust proceedings commenced

50. Details of any joint venture or other collaborative arrangements with any competitor

INTELLECTUAL PROPERTY AND INFORMATION TECHNOLOGY

Intellectual property

1. Details of all business names used by the Group
2. List, by product, of all third party and public domain intellectual property rights and technologies used in or required for developing, using, selling or copying the Company's products
3. Details of all IP rights registered or for which applications for registration have been made in the name of the Group, including patents, registered trademarks and service marks (including logos) and registered designs
4. Principal brand names and details of material unregistered IP rights owned by the Group, including unregistered trade and service marks (including logos), trading names, and design rights (including semi-conductor topography rights)
5. Details of any options, liens, charges or other encumbrances over or affecting the IP owned by the Group

6. Copies of all licenses agreements (whether oral or written, formal or informal) of IP or know-how granted to or by the Group and of any other agreements entered into by any member of the Group in relation to such rights (including consents, undertakings, settlement agreements, co-operation agreements, research and development agreements, etc.)
7. Copies of documentation (including copies of any relevant correspondence, pleadings and counsel's opinions) relating to any breach or alleged breach of any license or agreement referred to in 6 either by any member of the Group or any third party
8. Details of any challenges as to the validity, subsistence or ownership of any IP owned by the Group including any opposition proceedings brought by a third party in relation to any of the Group's IP
9. Copies of documentation (including copies of any relevant correspondence, pleadings and counsel's opinions) relating to any suspected or alleged infringement by a third party in the last three years of IP rights owned or used by the Group
10. Copies of documentation (including copies of any relevant correspondence, pleadings and counsel's opinions) relating to any suspected or alleged infringement by any member of the Group of any third party's IP or confidential information in the last three years

Information technology

1. Details of the current system used by the Group, including physical, network, systems and staff security

2. Copies of the security policy employed by the Group
3. Details of systems / processes in place to maintain the privacy/confidentiality of data
4. Details of all material IT owned by the Group (including hardware, software and networks)
5. Details of all material IT (both hardware and software) used by, or on behalf of, but not owned, by the Group
6. Details of any options, liens, charges or other third party rights over, or affecting, the IT owned by the Group
7. Copies of all material agreements and arrangements relating to IT entered into by the Group or under which the Group benefits (including software licenses, development, security, disaster recovery, EDI, escrow, computer bureau services, facilities management, web site, domain name and outsourcing agreements and arrangements), specifying in relation to software licenses, whether the relevant software is "off the shelf" or has been written or modified specifically for the company ("bespoke")
8. Details of any material disruption to the Group's operations during the last three years due to any IT security breach, failure or performance fault of any IT or any defective operation of any IT due to the occurrence or processing of any dates
9. Details of all domain names used by the Group
10. Description of the levels of support (technical, customer, etc.) the Group provides, if any

IT Asset Register

11. All Desktop – Make, model, serial number and date of manufacture
12. All Laptops - Make, model, serial number and date of manufacture

13. All Servers - Make, model, serial number, date of manufacture and function i.e. messaging server, file server
14. Network switches, routers, firewalls - Make, model, serial number and date of manufacture
15. Printers - Make, model, serial number and date of manufacture
16. Pabx / Telephony system – Make, model, date of manufacture

Messaging System

17. Technology i.e. MS Exchange or Lotus Domino
18. Schematic showing how mail is delivered from external to internal mail server
19. What mail client is used by users
20. How many active mailboxes on messaging system Users
21. How many users are there
22. What is the distribution of users per office / department /functional area
23. Are there any documented user profiles separating user classes based on systems used and function? If so please provide detail

Backups & Disaster Recovery

24. What backup technology is used i.e. Symantec or Net back-up
25. To what medium are backups performed to i.e.to tape or to disk. Please supply detail of backup cycles, media management and retention periods

26. Is there a documented backup policy and standard operating procedure? If so please provide copies

Network Structure / Domain

27. What authentication system is being used i.e. NT Domain, AD or other
28. Method of IP allocation and management – manual or DHCP
29. Method of name resolution – DNS and or WINS
30. Number of domain controllers
31. Detailed schematic showing all key network services and their relation to each other

Security & Anti-Virus (AV)

32. What AV system is being used for desktops and servers?
33. What perimeter security is used such as firewalls and intrusion detection?
34. What mail content filtering is being used?
35. What web content filtering is being used?
Facilities
36. Is the server room protected by solid brick walls?
37. Is there access control to the server room? What locking mechanism is used?
38. Power: detail of UPS's used in the server room including make, model, age, power rating and capacity
39. Power – is there a generator on site? Please detail make, model, age, power rating. Does it have a maintenance contract?
40. Power - is there an automated mechanism to switch to generator when mains power fails?

41. Temperature and Humidity control – what air conditioning and humidity control systems are in place?
42. Detail make, model, cooling rate i.e. BTU's
43. Fire suppression and prevention – what system is in place?
44. Is there an environmental monitoring system that monitors all the above and alerts of breaches in thresholds?
45. What kind of flooring is in the flooring i.e. ESD, raised, ceramic tiles?

Networking LAN / WAN

46. Schematic showing all network hubs / switches, name of the physical location i.e. accounts department, warehouse
47. What standard of Ethernet cabling is being used for the LAN i.e. CAT5 /CAT5E /CAT6
48. Is the cabling installation certified by the installer?
49. Schematic must be based on a scale building layout.
50. What internet connectivity exists? Detail bandwidth and connectivity type i.e. wireless, copper or fibre
51. Do you have connectivity to any remote office? Please provide details of connectivity model to remote offices

Telephony

52. What telephone system is being used i.e. Analogue / Digital /IPT
53. What type of cabling is installed for the telephone system?

54. Is the telephone cabling part of a structured cabling solution?
55. Is the telephone system under a maintenance contract? Please provide details

Vital Business Functions / Processes

56. What are the vital business functions i.e invoicing, manufacturing, stock control

Vital Business Systems

Detailed information for the following systems and any others that currently support vital business functions / processes:

57. Financial accounting systems
58. Payroll and wages systems
59. Time and attendance
60. CCTV
61. General access control
62. PLC / automated manufacturing systems

Suppliers & Service Providers

Comprehensive list of all key suppliers and service providers of all IT related equipment, products and services. Critical suppliers are:

63. Hardware vendors for all computers, servers, network equipment, printers and all other peripherals and ancillaries – All imported
64. Software and licensing vendors – All imported all OEM for servers and desktop / laptops

65. Service and support providers. Please include all details pertaining to contractual arrangement and supply copies of agreements where they exist

Licensing

66. Full list of all licenses currently owned. This must include all operating systems, office suites, special business system and any programs currently in use

IT Management

67. Current IT management structure?
68. List all personnel in IT detailing their skills / qualification levels and designated roles and responsibilities

ERP

69. ERP system being used
70. Version of the system is in use
71. Transferability of ERO system to purchaser with the purchase
72. Modules in use and how many users per module
73. Details of number of transactions per month per module
74. Number of master files in use and the number of accounts or codes per master file
75. Details of any third party products being used in conjunction with the ERP or are interfaced to the ERP
76. Details of where is the system hosted
77. Current status of system maintenance

78. ERP system renewal date
79. Details of annual Maintenance cost

ASSETS

Ownership and condition of assets

1. Details of any material assets used by the Group in the course of its business which are not included in the last audited accounts, except for current assets acquired since last reporting date in the normal course of trading
2. Details of any material assets used by the Group in the course of its business which are not owned both legally and beneficially by the Group
3. Capital expenditures and repairs of the Group for past three years, split by division and by maintenance and expansionary
4. Details of any third party rights and encumbrances, including options, mortgages and charges, on the undertaking or any of the assets of the Group
5. Current lists and details of vehicles and shipping vessels (cost, age, book value etc.)
6. Details of equipment leases or other property leases not covered in Property list below

REAL PROPERTY AND ENVIRONMENT INFORMATION

Property

1. Register of fixed assets for the past three years Depreciation policy for all assets in the Group
2. In respect of each property in South Africa owned or occupied by the Group, a completed copy of the "Property Particulars" appended to this list
3. Details of any material building works presently in progress at any of the properties including sums paid to date, the expected cost to completion and the expected date for completion
4. Copies of planning permissions for:-
   - Present use of each of the properties; and
   - Any development that has been carried out at any of the properties in the last three years
5. Details of any sharing of occupation and/or facilities between the Group and third parties
6. A list of any properties no longer owned or occupied by the Group where a Group member has a contingent leasehold liability, together with the current rent and expiry date of the lease
7. Details of all financing leases, sale and leaseback agreements and conditional sale agreements relating to property owned or occupied by the Group

Environment

Answers and copy documents relating to current or potential litigation or proceedings should be limited to basic factual information which is already known to both parties to the dispute and should not include any information or advice which is or might be subject to legal privilege

1. Environmental audit and inspection reports and monitoring and test reports (such as underground storage tank, groundwater, surface water, soil, sewer discharges and air emissions), whether performed internally or by third parties, and any related memoranda and correspondence
2. Description of operations involving use, emissions or discharges of hazardous materials or generation or disposal of waste. Details of relevant hazardous materials and wastes, including methods of handling, storage and disposal. Copies of disposal contracts and contractors' registrations
3. Details of any known exposure of employees to hazardous materials, noise, vibration or dust
4. Details of any known spillages or accidental discharges or emissions. Details of any known or suspected soil or groundwater contamination
5. Copies of environmental licences and any current applications for licences
6. Details of any known or suspected polychlorinated biphenyls ("PCBs") or asbestos
7. Details of any actual or threatened investigations, proceedings or claims by the relevant authorities or claims by third parties in relation to environmental or health or safety matters (including past investigations or claims) during the last three years

8. Any relevant material obligation in relation to recycling or recovery of packaging. If none, details of basis of exclusion or exemption. If any, details of steps taken to comply with the obligation and estimated expenditure over the next three years

EMPLOYMENT AND PENSIONS INFORMATION

Employees

1. List of all personnel employed by the Group, including persons who have accepted but not yet begun their employment or engagement or who are on leave (including maternity or sickness leave, including under health schemes) showing age; date of commencement of employment; number of years of continuous employment; salary or wages and other benefits (including bonus entitlements, benefits which are related to sales, profits, turnover or performance or which are otherwise variable (other than normal overtime); other arrangements for profit sharing and benefits received otherwise than in cash); notice periods; holiday entitlement; other relevant terms. Note that this information should not disclose employees' names (for data protection reasons)
2. Employee organization chart

3. Number of personnel in each department; for example, production, sales, and administration, broken down where possible by grade or job type
4. List of all consultants to the Group including names, functions, compensation and any other relationships to the Group or any of its officers and directors
5. Examples of each type of employment contract or other terms of engagement which are currently applicable and copies of all relevant staff or personnel manuals, including the HR remuneration policy and procedures manual
6. Details of any personnel who have handed in their notice or are under notice of dismissal (including, where known, the reason for the giving of such notice)
7. Details of any change made since the last accounts date in the wages or salary or other terms of engagement of any personnel, and of any such change (or negotiation or request for such a change) which is due or expected
8. Details of any grievance/disciplinary procedures
9. Details of any sickness/disability schemes
10. Copies of any share schemes, including option, incentive or profit sharing schemes, applicable to directors, employees or other personnel including related trust agreements and employee descriptive material
11. Details of share options or awards, or cash or other benefits dependent on share values of any member of the Group, granted to employees or former employees which remain outstanding
12. Particulars of any recognized trade unions; any applicable national or local trade union contracts or agreements; details of any collective bargaining agreement; details of any special redundancy arrangements established and details of any labor disputes in the last three years or current or threatened

13. Details of current or pending claims made by any director or employee or other personnel or ex-director or employee or other personnel (or any next of kin or dependents thereof) and of any such claims which have been threatened and of any such claims which have been made or settled in the last three years.
14. Details of, and copies of any correspondence relating to, any suspected or alleged breach by any member of the Group of its obligations concerning health and safety at work and any claims threatened or pending by any employee or other personnel or third party in respect of any accident or injury.
15. Details of any secrecy, confidentiality, non-disclosure and non-compete agreements with employees or other personnel or former employees or personnel that remain applicable
16. A list of all employees of the Group who are no longer employed by the Group, but continue to receive compensation and/or benefits, with copies of any severance agreements into which the Group has entered
17. Description of any training and development plans for employees
18. Description of the Group's leave policy

Pensions

19. Details and copies of relevant documents relating to any pension scheme(s) operated by any member of the Group including:
    - Trust deeds and rules;
    - Employee booklets and notices;
    - Names of the present trustees and actuary;

- Actuarial valuations, trustees' annual reports and annual audited accounts for the last two years;
- Details of the current rate of the employer's and employees' contributions to the schemes(s) and any proposed alterations to the current arrangements;
- Details of insurance premiums, taxes and expenses paid in relation to the scheme(s);
- A list of all existing members of the pension scheme(s) (and those likely to become members within the next six months) including sex, date of birth, date of joining the scheme(s), current pensionable salary, and any additional benefits granted or additional contributions made;
- Details of any ex gratia or unapproved or unregistered pension arrangements granted to employees;
- Confirmation that the scheme(s) are registered schemes and details of any reason of which the Group is aware as to why the pension scheme(s) may cease to be registered; and

20. A list of any employees of the Group not participating in the pension scheme(s)

TAX INFORMATION

Will need to be tailored for relevant local tax laws

Tax events since last reporting date

1. Details of any of the following which have happened since the last reporting date:
    - Any distribution declared, made or paid
    - Any disposal or event which will crystallise a material tax liability
    - Any material payment made which will not be tax deductible

General

2. Details of any preference share funding arrangements during the past 5 years
3. Details of any structured finance arrangements in place within the Group, including sale-and-leasebacks, forward purchase agreements, convertibles or any potential reportable arrangements
4. Details of instances where the Group has requested any tax rulings, and copies of any correspondence
5. "Stack-up" for the companies in the Group in respect of the items listed hereunder (which "stack-up" must reconcile to the last reporting date annual report for the Group):
    - Deferred tax asset
    - Deferred tax liability
    - Taxation (balance sheet)
- Taxation (income statement)
    - Tax reconciliation

Income tax

6. Tax computations and income tax returns (including supporting schedules) for the last five years of assessment of each of the Group
7. Tax assessments for the last five years of assessment of the Group
8. Provisional tax returns submitted for the last five years of assessment
9. Receipts in respect of payments made (provisional tax and upon assessment)
10. Tax computations for the most recent year of assessment (if the tax returns have not been lodged yet) for the Group
11. All correspondence with the Tax authorities for the last six years of assessment of the Group
12. Copies of objections and/or appeals lodged with Tax authorities in respect of assessments issued
13. Any documentation pertaining to any tax free reorganizations, tax rulings or tax clearances obtained by the Group in its last six years of assessment
14. Any documentation pertaining to significant acquisitions or disposals of any companies, businesses or assets by the Group in the last six years of assessment
15. Any queries raised or tax audits performed by tax authorities in the last five years of assessment of the Group, including any correspondence
16. Management letters from the auditors for years of assessment not yet assessed
17. Audit committee reports for years of assessment not yet assessed
18. Copies of material correspondence and/or tax opinions received from advisors
19. Details of any allowances that have been claimed in respect of learnerships

20. Details of inter-group loans and charges, including interest rates, current balance, etc.

Group relief

21. Details of any transactions that took place during years of assessment that have not yet been assessed, where the Group availed of any relief provided for company formation transactions, share-for-share transactions, amalgamation transactions, intra-group transactions, unbundling transactions and transactions for the winding up or liquidation and deregistration of entities

Value Added Tax ("VAT")

22. Copies of VAT returns, together with the supporting documentation in respect of the relevant VAT period, including VAT control account, per year for the last five years submitted to the Tax Authority by the Group
23. Details of specific VAT rulings issued by the Tax Authority in the last five years of assessment of the Group
24. Copies of VAT assessments issued by the Tax Authority for the last five years for the Group
25. All other notices, returns and correspondence with the Tax Authority (including queries raised by it) for the last five years for the Group
26. Proof that all vendors within the Group are registered for VAT
27. Receipts in respect of payments made for VAT purposes

Capital Gains Tax ("CGT")

28. List outlining the various classes of assets held by the Group (including corporeal and incorporeal assets). In this regard, we would require information relating to assets not typically found in the balance sheet, such as rights under off-balance sheet financing arrangements
29. Any material transactions which resulted in the disposal of an asset over the past three years
30. The Group's CGT policy, i.e. whether the Group has performed or is in the process of performing CGT valuations, each company's policy vis-à-vis adhering to the record keeping requirements prescribed by the Income Tax Act, etc.
31. Details of any CGT valuations made

Secondary tax on companies ("STC")

32. Copies of all STC returns submitted to the Tax Authority in respect of the last five years of assessment of the Group. Please provide details of any elections regarding the inter-group exemption from STC
33. Particulars of any dividends declared by the Group in the last five years
34. Receipts in respect of payments made for STC purposes

Import duties

35. Provide details of any import duties or any other customs and excise duties/taxes payable by any company within the Group

Distributions

36. Details of any share capital or other security issued as paid up otherwise than by the receipt of new consideration
37. Details of any part of the amount payable on redemption of any share capital or security at par which might be a distribution
38. Details of any share capital bought back over the last 12 months, including total number of shares held by a subsidiary as treasury stock

Tax indemnities

39. Details of any agreements or undertakings by which a member of the Group has undertaken to indemnify or compensate any other person for a taxation liability or has received any such right to indemnification or compensation

Employees tax

40. Select a sample of [number] employees from each management and wage level within the Group. The following documents in respect of these employees are required:
    - The general remuneration policy document governing the benefits that are/may be provided to the chosen employees, and the employees' tax consequences thereof.
    - The payslips of such employees for the year of assessment ended last reporting date.

- Employee tax certificates for the last reporting date
- Details of fringe benefits and the tax treatment thereof (e.g. remuneration schedules).
- Relevant correspondence to and from tax authorities and rulings received, if any.

41. Copy of the latest financial year-end employees' tax reconciliation submitted to tax authorities
42. Copies of the latest employee tax returns of the Group and copies of the corresponding employees' tax control account
43. Information regarding whether the Group was subject to any payroll investigations or audits conducted by tax authorities. Where such an investigation or audit has been performed, provide details regarding the findings of such an investigation or audit
44. Receipts in respect of payments made for employees tax purposes

Unemployment Insurance Fund, Skills Development Levy and Workmen's Compensation

45. Calculations of the Unemployment Insurance Fund, Skills Development Levy and Workmen's Compensation contributions for the last three years and review of all related documentation for the group companies

Exchange controls

46. Any exchange control consents obtained by the Group in the last five years

47. Details of any goods and services transferred by the Group to offshore group entities or vice versa during the last five years. Also details of other cross-border transactions entered into by the Group
47. Details of loans made to and by the group companies to offshore subsidiaries for the last five years
49. The relevant extracts of the annual feedback provided to the South African Reserve Bank in respect of offshore investments made by the Group
51. Provide details regarding any intellectual property transfers or licensing arrangements between the Group and offshore group entities as well as any licensing arrangements with third parties in other jurisdictions
52. Provide details of any transactions in terms of which offshore group entities transact with group entities and are paid fees, interest, royalties, etc. by any related parties or hold shares in any domestic entities

www.ingramcontent.com/pod-product-compliance
Lightning Source LLC
Chambersburg PA
CBHW031622210526
45464CB00004B/1702